Diva
nomi¢s

how to still be
fabulous when
you're broke

michelle mckinney hammond

Tyndale House Publishers, Inc., Carol Stream, Illinois

Visit Tyndale's exciting Web site at www.tyndale.com.

Visit Michelle McKinney Hammond at her Web site, www.michellehammond.com.

TYNDALE and Tyndale's quill logo are registered trademarks of Tyndale House Publishers, Inc.

Divanomics: How to Still Be Fabulous When You're Broke

Designed by Jessie McGrath

Edited by Katara Washington Patton

Published in association with the literary agency of Alive Communications, Inc., 7680 Goddard Street, Suite 200, Colorado Springs, CO 80920. www.alivecommunications.com.

Scripture quotations marked KJV are taken from *The Holy Bible*, King James Version.

Scripture quotations marked *The Message* are taken from *The Message* by Eugene H. Peterson, copyright © 1993, 1994, 1995, 1996, 2000, 2001, 2002. Used by permission of NavPress Publishing Group. All rights reserved.

Library of Congress Cataloging-in-Publication Data

McKinney Hammond, Michelle, date.
    Divanomics : how to still be fabulous when you're broke / Michelle McKinney Hammond.
        p. cm.
    Includes bibliographical references.
    ISBN 978-1-4143-3382-3 (sc)
    1. Christian women—Religious life. 2. Finance, Personal—Religious aspects—Christianity. I. Title.
    BV4527.M415 2010
    248.8′43—dc22   2009042957

Printed in the United States of America

16 15 14 13 12 11 10
 7   6   5   4   3   2   1

This is dedicated to all of those who have learned their hardest and sweetest lessons through the things that they've lost. May you not only find wisdom on the path to restoration, but also discover the most amazing truth of all—success in life is not found in who you become or the things you acquire. At the end of the day, who others become because of your presence will be remembered far longer than your fabulous suit or the house you live in. You are you, and the things you own are exactly that—merely things. Here's to not being owned by them and to the joy and peace that knowledge brings to your life.

❃

contents

Preface   ix
Acknowledgments   xi
Introduction   xiii

1. History Lessons   1

2. The Cold, Hard Facts   9

3. Looking in the Rearview Mirror   19

4. Get Real, Girl!   29

5. Moving Forward   37

6. Budget? What a Novel Concept!   45

7. The Benefits of Plastic Surgery   51

8. The Power of the Little Envelope and
   Loose Change   59

9. How to Say No and Still Look Beautiful   65

10. A Woman's Got to Have Priorities   71

11. The Fruit of Living Generously   79

12. The Power of a Social Life   87

13. The Secret of Community   93

14. Costco, Sam, and Other Famous Friends   99

15. Ask and You Shall Receive, but Bartering Is
    Even Better   105

16. Puttin' On the Ritz and Other Creative Options   111

17. Counting on the Kindness of Strangers   117

18. Damsels and Knights   123

19. Keeping Up Appearances   129

20. How to Go Shopping in Your Closet   135

21. The Secret to Self-Gratification   141

22. Coupons, Points, and Sales, Oh My!   149

23. There Is No Shame in Generics and Other Trade Secrets   157

24. Putting Your Best Face Forward   165

25. Sticking Close to Home   173

26. Cut the Fat   179

27. Rediscovering the Kitchen   187

28. More Than One Way to Skin a Chicken   193

29. Walmart, Tar-Jay, and Other Exotic Locales   199

30. Keep the Faith   205

31. Ask Daddy   213

32. Receive What You Believe   219

33. How to Live in a House That's beyond Your Means   227

34. Final Diva Thoughts   235

Notes   239
Additional Resources   241
About the Author   245
Additional Books by Michelle McKinney Hammond   247

preface

Warning: *If followed carefully, the information in this book will have you looking so good that no one will believe you need help. It would be wise to use all advice in moderation and at your discretion—depending on your audience, circumstance, and need.*

acknowledgments

A VERY SPECIAL THANKS to all the folks at Tyndale for letting me spread my wings. I'm excited about partnering and growing with you.

Carol Traver, you are my new BFF! What an inspiration you've been! Your wit has pushed me to new levels of crazy, but it's all good. (I think you missed your calling, but I'm selfishly glad you did.) I believe you are a kiss from God to me and the shot in the arm I needed at this time in my life. Thank you not only for believing in me, but for catching the vision and championing and inspiring me. You'll never know the full extent of your influence in my mind-set and my writing. Girl, we'll talk over calamari.

Katara Washington Patton, editor extraordinaire, thank you for your diligence in fine-tuning my offerings, keeping me honest, and making me look good. You rock! Only a great editor can correct you without making you feel stupid or insulted. You have finesse, my friend; I feel blessed to have you in my corner.

Beth Jusino, I am so going to miss you! You have been an amazing agent, so it is with a divided heart that I release you to go and do the rest of your life. Hmm, life . . . everyone should have one. I wish you the best.

Charlotte, thanks for giving me the idea for *Divanomics*; it's friends like you that keep a girl afloat.

Karen, thanks for all the encouragement and the list of resources you're always there to give—you are my she-ro!

Aunt Ernie, the quintessential "Auntie Mame," you've taken me around the world and taught me the value of living generously, finding a good bargain, and power shopping. What a woman! You are a precious gift to me.

Thanks to all those who have walked with me through one of the hardest times in my life. (You know who you are.) Your love has kept me strong, and I can see the finish line. I love you high, deep, and wide . . . nah, I love you more than that!

introduction

BEFORE WE BEGIN, let's get one thing straight—Suze Orman I am not! I love me some Suze; but truth be told, if I were her, I never would have ended up broke, broke, and even more broke than the previous two expressions. Are you getting that I wasn't looking so good on paper? But understand and know that I was still fabulous! Sad to say that where I landed is probably where a whole lot more people live than they care to admit. So know this up front: I can't tell you what stocks to buy, how to manage your portfolio, or what to do with your 401(k). (You still have one of those? Congratulations if you do.)

What I can tell you is my own story of a diva gone south, from fabulous to broke—although you'd never know it based on outward appearances. I can tell you how I got to broke and what it takes to make it when your taste and your lifestyle can no longer be sustained by your present budget. (Eww . . . I can't believe I said that word!) They say that hindsight is better than no sight at all, so let me say this: My girl Pamela always says, "If people knew better, they would do better," and hopefully that is true. So based on that premise, I am hoping that sharing my calamities with you and the solutions I've learned along the way will keep you from doing the same. However, if you're already in the same boat I almost sank in, perhaps my advice will keep you afloat until you make it to the other side.

But beyond keeping your head in financially trying times and looking fabulous in spite of it all, I believe that the good Lord wants us to not just *look* fabulous but *be* fabulous through and through. In order to do that, certain divine principles cannot be ignored. You know, divine is where the word *diva* really comes from—the root of *diva* in Italian is *divine*. (We sure got that twisted, didn't we?) By the world's definition, divas are highfalutin, difficult, self-indulgent, and totally impressed with themselves. I guess for every *yin* there is a *yang*, so let me set the record straight: In this book, we will deal with divas redefined to a higher standard of living, loving, and overcoming—financially, emotionally, relationally, spiritually, and otherwise. All of these things are intertwined. You cannot compartmentalize a woman's character. One bad habit affects everything else. Based on that knowledge, I had to dig deep to see that my financial dilemma went deeper than the bottomless pit my money had disappeared through. I had some internal issues that contributed to my financial demise, and I think that if you took a moment to reflect, you would agree the same was true for you.

So, first things first. As you journey with me on the road to recovery, know that you are not alone in your struggle.

Second, know it is not too late to recover. Third, recognize that whether your money issues come from legitimately falling on hard times or willful shopaholism (or a combination of both), there are valuable lessons to be learned that can actually work for you in the end. And last but not least, I can share a few secrets with you on ways to maintain your diva standards without spending money you don't have. I love that about God. Don't you? Somehow, someway, trials and tribulations all work out for the good if you let them. How? Well, if you embrace the truth, it will free you to learn from your mistakes and empower you to do the work you need to do to get the victory. You won't just get the victory, but you'll keep it—with change left over. And that, my sister, is a beautiful thing. On second thought, it's downright diva-licious!

Michelle McKinney Hammond

HISTORY LESSONS

THEY SAY NECESSITY is the mother of invention. And while some have been privileged to escape the hardships of life due to gleaning wonderful counsel or through the power of discerning observance, I have to admit, I graduated from neither college. Therefore I have learned everything I now know about money the hard way.

Blame it on my genes, ancestry, whatever. I was an international baby. My mother is from Barbados, West Indies. My father is from Ghana, West Africa. I was born in London, went to school in Barbados, and finally landed in Muskegon,

Michigan, after my mother married a rather tall, handsome American, whom I call my dad. With such exotic beginnings, there was no way I could ever have a taste for anything normal.

As the child of Third World parents along with one solid American, I somehow missed some of the lessons I should have absorbed. Generally speaking, those of African and West Indian descent are known for being very money conscious. Ever saving, making sure there was a stash left over for a rainy day and retirement, being careful never to "cut your coat larger than the cloth you own," as they used to say, our house never seemed to be in apparent shortage of funds. My parents did such a good job of supplying my every need that I assumed there would never be a shortage. The ever-indulgent Mr. McKinney (that would be my dad) was intent on my having everything I had written on my Christmas list, and so was I. Whatever he left off, Mr. Hammond, my biological father, would fill in the blanks. Imagine my pleasure as I sat opening present after present on Christmas morning and getting exactly everything I wanted. I was the envy of my friends.

Can you see how all of this generosity could give a girl the mind-set that no whim should ever be denied? This same thought process was only solidified as I grew up, made my own money, and found various and sundry ways of fulfilling my desires for all the niceties that life can supply. Somehow, I pulled it together and made it happen. Keep in mind that you are talking to a girl who had a fur coat in college, okay? And *I* bought it, thank you very much! It was not above me to work hard for what I wanted. Where there was a will, there most certainly was a way, and I was willing to put in the overtime to have my way.

Then, fresh out of college, I was caught up in the glamour of a fabulous advertising career. I was art director, copywriter, producer extraordinaire—flitting coast to coast producing television, radio, and print advertising for top-notch clients like McDonald's, Coca-Cola USA, and General Motors, to name a few. Flying all over the country, staying at the best hotels, and eating at the best restaurants on someone else's dime only fueled my love of the best life had to offer. Meeting celebrities, walking the red carpet, and being at all the soirees that others only dreamed of attending solidified my love for looking and playing the part. I learned all the top beauty and fashion secrets from the top makeup, hair, and fashion stylists in the business. *Dahling*, I was all that and a bag of chips . . . until I got fired. But for me, that was just a small hiccup in the scheme of life. It was on to the world of freelance, and I embraced being my own boss with abandon . . . until I got hit by a truck (literally). After three operations, a year and a half in bed, and the trial of learning how to walk again, I was still unwilling to release my diva status. You need to know I did not allow a cast that started at the top of my hip and extended down to my ankle to make me a fashion victim or stop me from getting my hustle on. In the words of the famous Tim Gunn, I knew how to "make it work."

Any diva worth her weight in gold knows how to make lemonade out of lemons. So, as I lay in bed, leg propped up in a cumbersome piece of equipment (I called it Harry since it was the only thing in my bed next to me), I wrote my first book, *What to Do Until Love Finds You* . . . and *bam!* I was back in the game. With one hit on my hands, I went on to pen thirty-four more books, have several best sellers, and sell over two million books. I became known as a relationship expert and singles guru, a champion of women's issues, and a life coach. Cohosting an Emmy award–winning talk show, traveling the globe to speak at conferences, I was flying high from Los Angeles to Africa and all points in between. I appeared on the covers of magazines, made guest appearances on shows like *Politically Incorrect* with Bill Maher, *The Morning Show with Mike and Juliet*—news shows, cable shows, you name it! I was on the diva track, moving and shaking. I had the loft apartment of my dreams on the river in downtown Chicago with my own office one floor up. I had wonderful jewels and clothing, along with two . . . *oops!* . . . three diva dogs. What more could a girl ask for? Believe me, during this stage in my life, if I wanted it, I found a way to get it.

When I saw Ed McMahon on television talking about declaring bankruptcy, I couldn't fathom how such a thing could be possible. How could a man who had obviously been a multimillionaire celebrity high roller with tons of money end up flatlining to nothing? But I found out. A funny thing happened on the way to my fabulous life that I thought would go on *ad infinitum*. I hit a dead end I didn't see coming.

Of course, all of this unchecked whimsy that I enjoyed, with no clear-cut checks and balances (and I do mean checks, literally), can only go so far. So here I sit at the end of my financial road, back at square one. Savings? Gone.

IRA? Bottomed out. (Isn't everybody's?) Creditors? We're on a first name basis. Shall I go on? How did I get here, you ask? Well, it's a long story that I'll share as we go along, but for now I'll give you the Cliff's Notes version. After making several business decisions that resulted in severe losses coupled with a parade of bad employee choices, my speaking engagements hit an all-time low, and my losses outweighed my gains. I had way more output than input going on. I was supplementing my losses with what I had left, but as you know, every good thing must come to an end. I had been able to stave off the impending flood but not outrun the downward tide. In short, I was just keeping afloat when a series of unexpected emergencies hit. (You know about the unplanned expenditures that happen in life, right? The car suddenly breaks down, medical hiccups . . . you get the picture.) Follow that up with the economy going south without checking with me to see if it was a good time, and I began to drown in the overwhelming tsunami of my debt. It was not pretty.

A funny thing happened on the way to my fabulous life that I thought would go on ad infinitum. I hit a dead end I didn't see coming.

The consequences of all that had transpired had finally caught up with me. As I sat looking at my profit/loss sheet for the year, the conclusion was in harsh black and white—all my hard work had netted me exactly negative $1,154. Every sign I had been avoiding now slapped me in the face. Negative! Can you believe it? Somewhere along the way I had missed the memo on how hard times were getting. Forging ahead with business as usual, I failed to pay attention to the bottom line until I was forced to. I had to reexamine what had brought me to this place. So if I may, allow me to share some diva-licious tidbits throughout this book that can make the difference between your navigating through the murky waters of lack and drowning. 'Cause believe me, sister, if you lose your boat, as opposed to your shirt, you still need to know how to swim!

DIVA REVELATION

Take a look at where your parents are financially right now. That is a picture of your financial future. If they are rich, that's good news. If they're not . . . well, that means you've got some work to do. For those of you who like to blame everything on Mama and Daddy, I believe that, since Jesus destroyed all generational curses on the cross, it's now up to you to break the cycle of generational habits (I really call it generational "stupid") that can affect your future. You do know that there's a difference between curses and habits, don't you? So take charge of your life! Learn from their successes as well as mistakes and make the lessons learned count.

Somewhere along the way I had missed the memo on how hard times were getting. Forging ahead with business as usual, I failed to pay attention to the bottom line until I was forced to.

WHAT'S A DIVA TO DO?

- Take a good, hard look at how your parents handled money. What was their mind-set? Spending habits? What was the outcome?

- Check yourself. In what ways are your money habits similar?

- List what has worked and what has not, as well as what you want your financial landscape to look like. Make a list of resolutions about how to move forward based on your observations and conclusions.

- Do not make unfair comparisons if your financial level is different from your parents', but remember that the fundamental issues remain the same. It's not what you spend; it's how you spend it!

2

THE COLD, HARD FACTS

I WAS BROKE. No ifs, ands, or buts about it. I was one fabulous, mink-wearing, diamond-flaunting, broke sister. If no one else believed it, I knew it. Once I allowed this knowledge to penetrate my hair weave and sink into my brain, it actually felt good to admit it. In fact, it was downright liberating. Mm-hmm, the truth will set you free, 'cause as long as you decide to stay in Egypt floating down a river called Denial, you will be a slave to what you refuse to acknowledge. You'll keep making the same mistakes. You'll still be robbing Peter to pay Paul or whomever in order to keep up your front while your rear is falling out. The downward descent will continue until you hit rock bottom and find yourself hopelessly stuck—stuck in your predicament, unable to make any move toward recovery. Hear me loud and clear: You cannot fix what you won't confess! So I decided that it was time for me to face the music and confess what I saw and knew about my financial situation; the song was not what I wanted to hear, but at least I could still hear *some*thing. When I made myself listen, I began to get a sense of direction. I needed to stop and take a good, hard look at where I was, and as embarrassing as it was, to seek wise counsel. They say that God takes care of fools and babies, and I am now totally convinced of that. Perhaps I wasn't ready to call myself a fool, but I was certainly feeling as helpless as an infant. *Waaah!*

Just as I sat looking over the fine mess I was in and trying to decide who to call, a friend called me. Although we were very close, I hadn't spoken to him in quite some time. We had the type of relationship that could handle the lapse. In one phone conversation, we could pick up right where we'd left off without a hitch or a question. Well, this particular morning I was anticipating him telling me about his last trip to some exotic locale, as he was given to bouts of climbing mountains in Peru or sailing around the world on a whim at any given moment. I had always seen him as a completely together brother who had no money worries at all. I knew he had recently left his job, and while I didn't know all of the particulars, I assumed that he had enough investments and other various and sundry means of income to keep him in the green and finance his impromptu adventures. Imagine my shock as he started sharing with me how he had run out of money, gotten behind on his mortgage and condo assessments—on and on his story went. I sat up. He was singing my song!

I realized that I was not alone! It had been hard to face my predicament at first because I had taken it so personally. I thought of myself as a bimbette when it came to money. I kept asking myself, *How could you let this happen?* I thought everyone was going to look down their noses at me from their lofty thrones of plenty; I thought people would celebrate my defeat if I let them know what was going on. Or worse yet, perhaps people would add insult to my injury by chiding me and listing all the things I had done wrong—as if I didn't already know those things. I was internalizing my shame to the point that I felt trapped, drowning in the panic of how I was going to meet all my financial obligations. I was past flailing. I was paralyzed and sinking like lead in a race to hit bottom—but my bank account had beat me to the chase.

I realized that I was not alone! It had been hard to face my predicament at first because I had taken it so personally.

Now, here was my dear friend openly telling me where he was and how he was tackling the problem. I was then able to open up and share where I was. As I dissolved into tears, telling him how afraid I was, he encouraged me not to give up, but he also gave me some sound steps to take. For the first time in weeks, I was able to breathe and have hope.

The cold, hard facts were that I had come to the end of myself and my own resources. There was nowhere else to go and no one else to borrow from. I had already dipped into the wallets of two relatives and had been unable to repay them, so I couldn't go back there. My credit was so frightening that there was no hope of a loan or a break anywhere else in sight. Plus, I just wasn't interested in borrowing another dime.

Enough was enough! Trust me, getting into more debt is not the way to get out of debt. I was behind on my mortgage, behind on my condo assessments, behind on my taxes, and my business line of credit was maxed out. As a matter of fact, the bank had done an assessment of my credit rating and pulled the line of credit for my check guarantee! I couldn't sell either of my condos because there was a special assessment on the building that the new buyer would expect me to pay before closing the deal. And, with plummeting market values, I would lose more than I would gain at this point. I couldn't rent out either place because the mortgages had ballooned, and I would never be able to rent them out at a price that would cover my costs. I would be left owing. On top of all of this, I wouldn't be able to rent a cheaper place to live to cut my expenses because you have to have good credit to get approved to rent a place. I was stuck between a rock and a hard place.

I was caught up in a vicious cycle of going nowhere fast. I was barely keeping abreast of the rest of my bills. Two mortgages, business expenses, employees . . . I was too big to operate as if I were small, but too small to operate as if I were big. Are you getting a picture of the mountain I was facing?

The truth of the matter was that I had been juggling for a long time, and now the plates were falling one by one. I had to stop, assess, and make some hard choices. My friend told me to be still, take a deep breath, and write down everything. Without a vision, the people perish.[1] But the vision needs to include where you presently are. Let's face it—in order to get directions from your GPS, you have to start with the place of origin. Next you have to have a clear picture of where you want to go. Once this information has been entered, the calculations begin to give you a clear route to your desired destination. Looking at where you are and how you got there can be the most difficult thing you will ever do, but it's the only way to get on the path to recovery.

Trust me, getting into more debt is not the way to get out of debt.

The Good Book says that you should know the state of your flocks and herds and also know who is among you.[2] Sad to say, at this point it was clear my flocks had run amok and my life and office were filled with great pretenders. So I decided first to clean house of all those who had been a drain on me financially, emotionally, and spiritually. At some point you have to learn not to take good-byes personally and understand that some folks are in your life for a reason or a season. So if I couldn't find a reason for someone to remain in my employ, it was time to let go and move on. This was hard, but necessary. There were friends who were negative, negative, negative . . . did I say negative? They drained me of my energy, my time, even my confidence, which affected my decisions and cost me. Some were just needless distractions, which can seem harmless, but anything that diffuses your focus is detrimental to your success. People who take more than they give can be economically distressing, or bad distractions at best. It is far better to align yourself with those who add to your life—wisdom, finance, encouragement, something of value that you can use to move forward in life.

After I assessed my relationships and cut some ties, I then moved on to the more black-and-white issues—the real numbers of what I owned and what I owed. I decided to focus on what I had first before I went on to the less pleasant truths.

My car was paid for. I had two pieces of property that should increase in value if I were able to keep them and if a "change" ever came to America. (Real estate is believed to be positive debt because it appreciates, though I was beginning to feel that by the time you were done with taxes and ever-climbing assessments, coupled with special assessments, owning a condo was highly overrated and much more negative than positive, but that was just my humble opinion.) I tried to maintain an optimistic point of view about home ownership. "This is a good thing," I muttered. Perhaps the operative word here is *home*. I've decided it is far better to own a house and rent a condo. With a condo you are at the whim of how others spend your money to maintain the building. With a house it's all yours—just a little food for thought.

Now for the unpleasant part: The rest of what stared up at me from the paper was a pile of negative debt I had to address. It was going to be an interesting journey, but I was determined to move past where I was to greener pastures and reclaim my flock.

It's up to you, however you want to do it—whether you focus on what you have first or deal with things all together—but the bottom line is that it's time to face the music. Look at the numbers in black and white. Some of you will be surprised to find out how much of your stuff still belongs to the bank, Mr. Visa, Miss MasterCard, your friends AmEx and Discover, or whomever you've been borrowing from.

Remember, the truth is the light, girl. Pull out some paper and a pen or pencil and take realistic stock of where you are. Even if you're not broke, you should do this, 'cause if you can avoid a problem before you get to it, you should. Make a list of all your stuff. Everything you have, everything you owe. Savings, IRA, investments, checking accounts, credit card balances—you name it, write it down. Put what is in the black on the right side of your sheet and what is in the red on the left. Take a good, hard look. Total up what you owe. Whew! Uh-huh, that's what I said.

Remember, I'm taking this journey too. (You don't think I just shared *all* of my business with you for the fun of it, do you?) The journey is always easier when you have company. If you promise to stay honest with me, I'll keep it real with you, and you know what? I believe we'll be able to get through this together.

DIVA REVELATION

When you decide you are no longer married to your image, you will be free to be real with yourself and others. You will be able to face the cold, hard facts. Authenticity opens doors you would never expect and will get you the help that you need. However, be sensitive as to who can handle what you are sharing. Not everyone can handle the truth of hardship. If they can't, give grace for their humanity and their sense of feeling helpless and don't hold it against them. When you see their eyes glazing over, or see them backing up, change the subject and move on to lighter fare.

WHAT'S A DIVA TO DO?

- Make a realistic assessment of your situation.

- Reach out to loved ones who can support you emotionally and perhaps assist materially or with advice.

- Seek financial counseling.

- Grab a copy of *The Total Money Makeover* by Dave Ramsey.

- Go to SuzeOrman.com under "Suze's Tools" and check out her "Expense Sheet." It will help you see exactly where all of your money is going—painful, but good.

3

LOOKING IN THE REARVIEW MIRROR

HOW DOES A DIVA get herself in such a pickle? Well, there are many roads that lead to a place called Debt and Despair. It's called the lust of the eyes, the lust of the flesh, and the pride of life.[1] Uh-huh, debt and despair happen when our eyes are bigger than our budgets, our flesh is louder than our common sense (though I've learned sense is not common), and our pride feels the need to sell tickets we can't really cash. Add to this equation a lack of knowledge—which will always cause one to err and make costly mistakes—and you've got one huge problem. Couple that with a passionate love of shoes, fashion, and fine dining, and you're in big trouble! Try to run a business on top of that, and it's over, my friend.

As we discovered in the previous chapter, the first step to recovery is admitting where you are and facing the cold, hard facts. Confession is good for the soul and the pocketbook. The next step has got to be reviewing where you've been. Those who ignore history are destined to repeat it. I have to say, I've gotten out of debt several times. The big question now is, why did I return? What was it on the inside of me that had not reconciled some core truths that could keep me on the right side of my finances? There were two things I needed to look at closely: how I handled my personal money and how I handled my professional business. There were differences but also similarities. One cannot compartmentalize basic character, so certain parts of our personalities and decision-making processes spill over into every arena of our lives and cause the same problems on all fronts.

Those who ignore history are destined to repeat it.

It's been said that the devil is in the details, and trust me, if he runs around unsupervised, you'll have a big mess on your hands. Admittedly, I am a happy, sanguine temperament, a visionary, creative type. In my psyche, life is a constant celebration. Everything has to be fun, and when it's not, I abdicate. Details are not fun for me. They cause my eyes to cross and my brain to lock. Most people see me as being very disciplined because I've written more than thirty-four books in ten years, but what they fail to understand is that writing those books was fun for me. That's why I believe everyone should do what they were created to do (but life purpose and what makes us excellent are a whole other subject in another book). Right now, we are reviewing the steps one takes to get to a place called Broke.

So I asked myself, *How did you get here, girlfriend?* Well, I have a friend who always says good-bye with the same phrase: "Go handle your business." As I looked in the rearview mirror and studied my past, I realized that between juggling my personal business and my *business* business, I had not been handling *my* business—personally or professionally. All the warning signs were there, lights were flashing, creditors were calling, and I was still sailing down a river called Oblivious. I was still shopping, eating out, carrying on as if nothing were wrong, until all my past sins, as well as the sins of those I had employed, piled up and created an embankment I could no longer get around.

In the middle of a birthday dinner I was throwing for a friend, a rather obnoxious sheriff served me an eviction notice because I was behind on my condo assessments. You'd better believe I was hot under the collar and called an attorney cousin of mine to complain and get her counsel. I tearfully explained to her that I had spoken to the building manager and the attorney they had given my bill to and assured them I would be able to settle my debt at the end of the month. When I got my check, I asked for the attorney's number and address to let him know the check was on the way. I never received the information. I traveled, came back home, and

It's been said that the devil is in the details, and trust me, if he runs around unsupervised, you'll have a big mess on your hands.

was greeted with papers summoning me to court. Obviously, my condo's management company had proceeded to serve me before I'd even made the call about the check. Instead of sympathy for my story and the sad turn of events, my cousin scolded me and responded with, "When are you going to stop expecting other people to take care of the things that are your responsibility?" Despite the facts and history of how this particular incident had transpired, I saw the truth in the middle of her hurtful tirade—I had abdicated responsibility in several areas of my life and my business, and now all the chickens were coming home to roost at the same time. It reminded me of the Scripture in Lamentations (appropriate title) that basically says, "She did not consider her future, therefore her fall was terrible."[2]

You see, in the past I had always found a way to recoup, dance around debt, find creative ways to still have everything I wanted, and stay ahead of my obligations. I never considered that you could only dance so long before you ran out of breath and money. I didn't count on the world going broke around me or trends changing. I kind of thought that things would continue as they always had with streams of income miraculously bursting forth in the nick of time to shore up my expenditures.

But alas and alack, the totally unexpected happened: markets crashed, banks ran out of money, the country's finances tanked, and we all ran aground together. All of a sudden I was grounded with no work for months. Yes, panic had spread to the rest of the world from the financial fallout, and people were hoarding the few shekels they had. Even folk in the church. Programs were cut, and no one was buying books the way they used to. It affected my bottom line quick, fast, and in a hurry. It was downright excruciating. The few speaking engagements I managed to get didn't pay, or their checks bounced, and the harsh reality that God was no longer going to rescue me from myself began to sink in as my output exceeded my input until there was nothing to put anywhere anymore.

The end of the matter was simply the period of a long sentence that had begun long before, a slow build, so to speak. It had taken me some time to realize that I was quickly approaching a year with a mysteriously sparse speaking schedule. After a series of events, I discovered that my assistant at the time had not been responding to booking requests or returning the calls of those who sought my services. In the middle of this, my accountant took me to dinner to tell me to stop spending. However, he failed to tell me what to stop spending and how much. Then the phone calls started. Bills that I had assumed were paid were not. Extraneous bills that could have been paid in installments had been paid in full, leaving no money to "spread the wealth" among those that remained to keep the collectors at bay. On top of this, he hadn't done my taxes for two years! When I asked why, he simply said, "You don't have the money to pay them." Fancy that. Just when I thought things couldn't get any worse, they did. One day after having my debit card declined for a mere forty dollars (I knew I'd had much more than that when I checked the balance that morning), I caught several large forged checks to the tune of several thousand dollars being written on my account pending before they cleared. (I don't believe it was my accountant. The checks were generated from a city I had visited.) On that note, I shut down every account and decided it was time to own my stuff and handle my accounting myself in order to figure everything out. I let go of my accountant since there was nothing to account for, sat in the middle of the floor looking at all the paperwork around me, and wept. It was like a bad pileup of events at the corner of Confusion and Wipeout.

So let's do the math and consider the bottom line of this all-too-common dilemma. I was one clueless diva running unchecked when it came to my spending habits—after all, I had never had to rein in my spending before, but this was a different day, a different time. Little did I know, all it takes is one incompetent assistant and failure to micromanage to set you on a course to ruination. Add one accountant not communicating, not paying your bills, and not taking care of business, plus an adjustable mortgage blowing up in your face along with staggering special assessments on both of your properties, the IRS breathing down your neck for two years of back taxes, minus the work that is your bread and butter, and you're finished. Whew! I had had all the above piled on top of my own bad habits. Now, a year later, my bad decisions and failure to know what was going on, coupled with a crippled economy, threatened to wipe me out in an avalanche of debt. I was like the lady in the commercial saying, "Help! I've fallen, and I can't get up!"

Looking back, I could see where my lack of paying attention to details and warning signs had caused my demise. My cousin was right. At the time, I hated her for it, but the truth is the light. I could blame it on being too busy to pay attention or the failure and incompetence of others, but there were still more fingers pointed back at me. I was the common denominator in all of my woes. I couldn't blame my empty calendar on my assistant who didn't return calls the year before. I should have asked more questions and investigated why I had no speaking engagements. I couldn't blame my accountant for not doing my taxes for two years. I should have moved on to someone who would do them. Are you getting my drift?

Far too many times we are more volunteer than victim for the stuff that happens to us. I had "erred for lack of knowledge," as the saying goes. What you don't know can and will hurt you. I had just learned that lesson and a few more the hard way. Ignorance was not bliss, an acceptable excuse, or an escape from the consequences of my fiasco. Just because I ignored the facts didn't mean they were going away. They were there staring me in the face, hitting me where it hurt—in my wallet. What was a diva to do? The only thing a diva could—keep her head up, learn the lessons, and consider how to move forward.

DIVA REVELATION

Alright, alright, everybody from President Obama to your mama has lectured you on responsibility. There's no way around it; no excuses; no ifs, ands, or buts. You've got to do the work to get the results you want. No pain, no gain. So bite the bullet, my sister. You may hate it, but taking responsibility and staying on top of details is crucial to your existence and your success. So pull up your big-girl undies and deal with it! Take a hard-core look back down the road that led you to your current state—whether that's a good place or not. Be honest with yourself—it's the only way you're going to get a handle on what's keeping you from financial liberation!

WHAT'S A DIVA TO DO?

- Write down your specific circumstance. Where are you financially? Pretend you are the president addressing the country about its fiscal state, except the "country" is your house, and we're dealing with your wallet and bank accounts. Write a speech to inform us of what is going on in "your country" fiscally; explain how you got there, what needs to be done to restore health to the "nation," and how you would like to move forward.

- Clarify where you missed it in judgment. When did your finances go south? What did you buy that you shouldn't have? What made you indulge in certain expenditures that you shouldn't have? What signs did you ignore? Where were you emotionally? What were you trying to accomplish when you bought what you did? What was the outcome of your spending?

- As best you can, list what you could have done differently and what needs to be done now.

4

GET REAL, GIRL!

HOW TO MOVE FORWARD.... The answer was not as simple as getting another book contract or trying to get more speaking engagements or even considering doing other freelance work for my old job. These were Band-Aids. It was time to go deeper to changing some habits. It was time to take realistic stock of what I had and what I didn't have. As much as I had tried to avoid a truth check, it was time for exactly that. I had to face my reality and actually do something about it. Admitting what I had done was only the beginning, because admission alone achieves nothing. It was time to embrace my part in the mess I found myself in and to do what I had to do to create a new truth—one with less debt and no more repeat performances of the same tragic tale.

One of the truths I had to deal with was the same one I avoided when it came to my weight. Once upon a time I could eat whatever I wanted and not gain a pound. Now when I look at a piece of cake, I could just as well just rub it right on my hips, 'cause that's where it's going to land once I put it in my mouth. This is a fact I refuse to accept, and I pay for it every time my dress size goes up another notch. The same is true of my finances. I did not have a bottomless bank account or the metabolism of a sixteen-year-old, and everything I spent or ate would be accounted for one way or another. It was time to get real. To further remind me of how the consequences of my habits could not be hidden or denied, while applying for a loan modification on my mortgage, I had to fill in the *real* figures I was dealing with.

Now, as scary as the numbers of what I owed looked, it was strangely interesting that once they were written down on the application, they didn't look as insurmountable as they had been in my head. Perhaps this is why the Bible says to write the vision and make it plain so that you can run with it.[1] Adding everything up and looking at it on paper made it clearer to see what I owed and what I needed to do to get back in the black.

My next step was to be realistic about what it was going to require to get myself out of this financial quagmire. I was reminded that a drowning man who keeps flailing and splashing cannot be saved. He is likely to drown his rescuer along with himself. He literally has to relax and stop fighting in order to be pulled to shore. I know that anytime you make a decision based on fear, anger, or pride, you will always make the wrong decision. I had to still my mind, heart, and spirit in order to receive the wisdom I would need to move forward. "What to do, Lord?" I whispered. "You've got to show me the way out."

The first thought that came to me was, *Understand the times.* Again I thought about my struggle with weight. Just as I had to come to grips with a changing body and the reality that I had to adjust the way I ate, the answer was clear. The times must dictate our approach to the issues in our lives. It was clear, given the financial landscape, that it was not a good time to be a spendthrift. I could no longer spend the way I used to. I could no longer take for granted that money or opportunities would fall out of the sky; everyone who had any sense was tightening their belts.

During this quest to learn from my mistakes, a particular phrase from a sermon hit home. J.R., our assistant pastor, was teaching on idolatry. "I'll tell you how you can spot the idols in your life," he said. "What did you spend your last five hundred dollars on?" Ouch! In that moment I knew that shoes and jewelry were my idols. It didn't stop there. Outward appearances were my idols too. Good food, taking exotic trips . . . they were all idols. None of them were terrible in themselves; it was their hold on me that was bad. I know that God doesn't have anything against us wanting to look good, and I'm sure He doesn't have anything against a good meal, either. It's not us having desires that is the problem;

it's a problem when our desires have us, when they reign and rule over us and the good sense God gave us. The reality I had to face was that I could no longer do life, and the pursuit of the things I wanted, in the same manner. It was time to let my idols go.

It was time to grow up and deal with the fact that I was no longer a child to be indulged. I had to become mature, be a responsible adult, put away childish ways, and approach my circumstances with maturity and balance. God wasn't out to do me in and deprive me. He wanted me to be free to enjoy the gifts He gives without buyer's remorse and the stress of unmet obligations. It was possible, but it would take discipline. Eww! I really hate that word. But it is absolutely necessary, even for a happy sanguine like myself.

It's not us having desires that is the problem; it's a problem when our desires have us, when they reign and rule over us and the good sense God gave us.

Could it be that this was what this whole exercise was all about? As I examined the traits of my friends who were not in my predicament, a few things stood out. They were all very anal about details, very disciplined people, very deliberate in what they chose to do with their time as well as their money.

I recognized, as I considered their lifestyles, that money was not the only thing I wasted. Truly my dalliances into all types of distraction keep my life interesting and entertaining for the most part. This always made me wonder if my more disciplined, detail-oriented friends were having any fun, but now in light of my present circumstances, I realized that there was a happy place between regimented discipline and spontaneous whimsy that was looking more and more desirable as the days went by. This was sobering, to say the least. A part of owning where I was had to include recognizing the part I'd played in my own undoing. But beyond that, I was trying to understand how I was going to correct the damage. Habits had to be changed, which meant attitudes and mind-sets had to be adjusted. I could no longer compare being disciplined to the way I felt about eating steamed broccoli—boring and uninspiring. Let's face it: The upside of eating steamed broccoli is that it is good for you. I had to learn to enjoy things that were good for me—good for my life and my budget. I could no longer indulge myself in every whim and fancy just because I wanted to have some enjoyment; I was realizing that true enjoyment could be found in doing what was good for me. The days for overindulgence were over. Times had changed. Life as I had known it had changed, and I had to change with it. Change is hard, but change is also good for you. I think that God in His infinite wisdom allows us to come to the end of ourselves in order to make us yield to a new direction and embrace change.

Something about us—whether we are divas or not—is that we are resistant to change. Though we desire to leave Egypt like the stubborn Israelites forced to make bricks without straw for the ruthless Pharaoh[2] (everyone has read the book of Exodus or seen *The Ten Commandments*, right?), the fear of the unknown often makes us settle for the very leeks and onions we hate and complain about. And so God allows our situations to become downright uncomfortable and unbearable in order to force us out of the places where we've entrenched ourselves. Though we go kicking and screaming, eventually we see the light and take the credit for the change He orchestrated. 'Tis true more often than not.

It's important to note that what we focus on during the times of transition is what we get. What we believe is going to be translated through our attitudes and the things we say, which will drive our actions and become habits that affect our characters and determine our destinies. So on that note, my friend, please know and understand that we are the masters of our ships, and God has given us the wheel. He is the wind, the sea, the sun—all of the elements that have greater power—and yet He has handed us the ability to work in concert with Him. It is our free choice that gets us in trouble. When we follow His direction, we land safely at our desired destinations. When we work against the flow of what He is trying to accomplish in our lives, we run the risk of drowning or running aground. It was clear to me that the tide was changing and it was up to me which direction I wanted to take. It was going to take some doing, but I could eventually arrive at a country called Free. I was ready. I couldn't get started fast enough. All I knew was that I had no intentions of returning to Egypt. I had already been there, and I had taken enough pictures of what debt looked like to last a lifetime. It was time to get rid of the idols and head to the Promised Land.

Please know and understand that we are the masters of our ships, and God has given us the wheel. He is the wind, the sea, the sun—all of the elements that have greater power—and yet He has handed us the ability to work in concert with Him.

DIVA REVELATION

You are the only one who can clear off your altar. No one else can be blamed or controlled when it comes to your life but you. It's a bitter pill to swallow, but the truth will make you well. Hopefully you will draw strength from it and renew your mind so that your life can be transformed. Of course, when you want change to occur in your life, it is entirely up to you. If you haven't fully committed to changing your financial path or learning from your mistakes, do this little exercise. Close your eyes and imagine that it's five years from now and your finances are in even worse shape than they are right now. . . . Oh, quick, open your eyes before you hurt yourself! Hopefully that will be enough incentive to do what you need to do to get on the path to healthy finances. If that's you, I will meet you in the next chapter.

WHAT'S A DIVA TO DO?

- List your idols (your bank and credit card statements will give you a clue); think about the reasons you have spent beyond your means. You may even list the things you spent your last five hundred dollars on.

- Clarify why these things are important to you. Go back to when they first became important to you. What were you thinking? Why did you want these things?

- Now put things into perspective and list how necessary these items are to your world. What would you be missing if you didn't have these items or indulge in them anymore?

5

MOVING FORWARD

LET ME JUST SAY THIS: Once you've made a decision that everything must change, everything and anything will rise up to oppose your new resolve. There will always be one more sale, one more deal you can't resist, one more opportunity you just *have* to take. One more . . . one more . . . It's kind of like when you decide to go on a diet, you try to eat everything you just know you're going to miss . . . mm-hmm. The same thing happens when you decide to become financially responsible. Such a deal! Everything beckons you to make one last purchase. And if you give in to the temptations of the deals right before your spending "diet," all of the little deals will have risen to another mountain of accumulated expenditures; and this money, too, would have been better spent on a bill that had been crying out for attention for quite some time.

It's true—bad habits are hard to break. Therefore, you have to set boundaries for yourself. Put measures in place to keep you on track; otherwise, you are sure to be distracted. Make attainable goals for yourself that won't make you feel like you're in prison. Maybe you won't buy another new thing until you pay off one of your small bills. You might find you feel so good about being free from a small part of your debt that you may be inspired not to buy anything and move on to getting rid of the next bill. Not only are you going to have to get real with yourself and God, but you are going to have to get real with other people—other people who will keep you accountable. I personally have an inner circle of twelve friends, with six of those being the main ones who speak into my life consistently. The others I touch base with, but not as regularly because of distance. When seeking advice for your life, you should always select someone who is successful at doing what you want to achieve. Ask questions. Share your situation and take serious note of his or her feedback. Afraid of your closest friends knowing the intimate details of your life? Then seek professional financial counseling. Some credit cards such as American Express offer you this service for free depending on your card status. This is what these people do for a living! They will give you the 411 on what to do straight with no chaser. Or read books by the ones who have been proven and respected authorties—Suze Orman, Dave Ramsey. There's a plethora of them. But you will still need someone who loves you to watch your back and walk through the day to day with you. Choose someone who can speak the truth to you in love and not make you feel condemned if you mess up but keep you on point just the same. It's kind of like going to Weight Watchers. When you know you have to face the scale, you stick to the program! So there you have it.

Now that you've looked at the bottom line of what you have and what you don't have, taken a good look at what brought you to this place, and committed to changing, you need to write out a plan of how you are going to tackle what is before you. Don't despise small beginnings. Remember the question, how do you eat an elephant? And the wise response, one bite at a time. The natural inclination is that if we can't do everything about something, then we tend to do nothing. But if you watch a stopped sink with a dripping faucet long enough, you will see it begin to fill and overflow. Little by little is the name of the game.

It's true—bad habits are hard to break. Therefore, you have to set boundaries for yourself.

In order to move forward, you've got to have a plan. No one goes on a trip without checking a map and planning the route. When you can see where you're going and have a time-line, it makes it easier for you to stay on course and enjoy the journey. Did I mention this was a journey?

Oh yes, my dear, this is a journey to a better you. I think in God's divine mind He knows that some lessons are better learned over time. That way the knowledge is ingrained, put into practice, and sustained permanently. For every quick fix, you have a repeat offender because they didn't feel enough misery to learn the lesson. It has been scientifically observed that most people who win the lottery are broke within a year. Why? Because they aren't used to having money. Subconsciously it is more comfortable to unload the money by giving it away and buying a bunch of stuff in order to get back to where they were originally. The poverty mentality is still inside of them even though they now have great riches. I am convinced that when God doesn't get you out of something, it's because He is trying to get something out of you; He is trying to teach you something— something that will stick because of the time and energy you spent enduring the pain and learning the lesson.

When you can see where you're going and have a timeline, it makes it easier for you to stay on course and enjoy the journey.

It is important not to despise the process as we go through life, whether it's a lesson on finance, romance, or all the other ways you do life. There is no getting around the lesson. If you skip the class, you will be back to take it again. Therefore, I say bite the bullet, do the homework, and learn to enjoy it. When we embrace the lessons that life is trying to teach us, we come out the better and richer for it. The knowledge that we acquire along the way preserves us and gives us the sustained victory we all want so badly.

When I was a little girl, I used to watch my grandmother process meat. She had this grinder that she would pass large chunks of meat through. It would be practically liquid when it came out the other end. Then she would add seasonings and preservatives and repackage it. This way it had a longer shelf life than it did in its original form. Truly we are works in progress. As we allow ourselves to be broken down, seasoned, and renewed, our longevity is ensured. This means that our short-term thinking has to be put to rest. We have to have a long-term mind-set. The choices you make today will affect your tomorrows when you least expect them to. The temptation to grasp at straws of temporary gratification must be corralled in order to achieve future goals—that would be mainly security and peace of mind. Amen to that!

I was now ready for the surgery. Whatever it was that was in me that got me to this place, I wanted it gone so I could get on with the business of living a life unencumbered by debt.

I was ready to plan my work and work my plan, but in order to do this, I needed to surround myself with wise counsel. Obviously my way of doing things before wasn't working. As I always say, the definition of insanity is continuing to do the same thing and expecting different results. It was time to flip the script on how I viewed and treated money. Step by step, inch by inch, I was ready to face my foe and put it to rest once and for all. Now that I was no longer in a broccoli mentality about dealing with money matters, I was ready to dig in. I figured that, with a healthy heaping of butter, I would learn to enjoy the flavor.

DIVA REVELATION

Don't take the lesson personally. This thing is called life, and for those who make any kind of positive impact, it is a process of growth. For every successful person you'll ever meet in life, they've got stories about the setbacks and the trials they endured to get to where they are right now. The richest people have suffered loss and learned how to sustain their wealth through trial and error. It's not making the mistake that makes you a fool; it's making the mistake and never learning from it. So don't cry over spilled milk. Clean it up and get a safety lid next time around.

WHAT'S A DIVA TO DO?

- Make a list of your debt. Now we're getting more specific about exactly where you need to eliminate or trim the fat. This is not just credit cards; this is everything—what you owe Aunt Sarah, the cleaners, everybody. Line them up in order of the largest amounts first. You need a bottom-line figure that you are now going to apply yourself to reducing.

- Prioritize your debt reduction. (Get rid of the credit cards with the highest interest rates first.)

- Create a goal time for getting out of debt, and write out your schedule and plan. (More on this later.)

- If you didn't do it before—you really should check out the "Expense Tracker" on SuzeOrman.com.

6

BUDGET? WHAT A NOVEL CONCEPT!

FACE IT, GIRL: A woman's got to have boundaries! We may be born free, but you have to learn to rein your impulses in. I learned a long time ago that I cannot go to the grocery store without a list. If I do, I come home with everything I don't need and more. Everything that caught my eye or hit my fancy or looked *slightly* delicious got thrown in the basket. In retrospect, I would arrive home with none of the things I needed and a lot larger bill than I had anticipated to boot. Ah, but when I went with a list, I came out the better for it. The same principle could easily be applied to money. There is safety in boundaries. They keep you disciplined and free from excesses you really don't need.

I would marvel when I went shopping with my friend Karen. She would try on all this great stuff, pile it up on the table, and then begin to calculate what it all added up to. If it surpassed the limit she had set for herself, she would put it back. "Mm-hmm, I love it, but it's over my budget," she would say, pursing her lips. She would give the garment one last glance of appreciation before putting it back on the rack. "B-b-b-but it's on sale! Such a deal!" I would squeal. "Yeah, but I just can't do it right now," she would sigh. "You're a better woman than me," I would mutter. And it was true. I was in debt, and she wasn't. She knew her limitations. She chose to set her limits before the limits were set for her. Smart cookie. Talk about self-empowerment.

Yes, that is exactly it! Setting the limits is not about deprivation; it is about empowering you not to cut your coat bigger than the cloth you have, as the old folks used to say. In other words, it is far better to live below your means with dignity than to live beyond your means in embarrassment. Believe me, all of your excess will eventually catch up with you and poke you in the gut like a long-lost friend. Like the devil who comes for payday in the fable "The Devil and Daniel Webster," debt has a long memory and does eventually become extremely insistent on collecting its due. When you start piling up envelopes because you can't deal with opening them, you have a problem. You see, it's most

There is safety in boundaries. They keep you disciplined and free from excesses you really don't need.

likely that the greatest secret to living a fabulous life is living a stress-free life, and stress-free is not worrying about bill collectors calling you or overdue notices showing up in your mailbox

Think of it this way: You can't pay for peace, okay?! And most certainly, money can't solve everything. There are many wealthy people running around stressed out about all the other areas of their lives that are beyond their control or the power of their wallets to fix. *In other words, it* But this is all about taking control of what *is far better to live* we can master, and like it or not, that means *below your means* you have to have a . . . I know, girl, it's even *with dignity than* hard to say it . . . b-b-budget. There, you've *to live beyond* said it. *your means in*

You have to have a new attitude toward *embarrassment.* having a budget. You see, a budget will mess with your pride; that's why we don't like budgets. Budgets are like girlfriends with their hands on their hips telling you as they swivel their necks, "Now you know you cannot have that!" "Chile, you know you better put that back!" I can't stand it when my friend Valencia gives me a reality check. After I've thrown her a dirty look, she always says, "Hey, I'm just trying to help a sistah out!" To which I reply, "Thanks for sharing."

But no matter who you try to fool, a budget is still there after everyone you can hide the shopping bag from has left. Your budget is there staring you in the face, pointing to the bottom line. So you need to embrace the fact that a budget is your best friend. It keeps you safe. It keeps you from buyer's remorse (yes, some people actually have that!) and bills you don't want to open. See, peace is a beautiful thing when you open a bill with the full confidence that you can pay it and pay it on time. Whether you've been to dance school or not, it's no joke trying to tap-dance around debt. You can only pretend to know what you are doing for so long. You cannot remain clueless about what you have or don't have. It's like building a house without counting the cost or taking an inventory of your materials to make sure you have enough to finish what you've started. Now fancy that! You're halfway finished with the first floor and realize you ran out of stuff before you could put on the roof. The first hint of rain is the beginning of the end for you. You are unprotected, and all that you've built is sure to be spoiled. So much for not knowing what you're working with.

Far too many people have too much month left over at the end of their paycheck cycle. You know what I'm talking about—that's when you've spent everything before your next pay cycle, leaving you behind in your obligations. So take a deep breath and repeat after me: "I will be realistic about my finances. I promise myself I will not spend more than I have." Wow! That is huge! In an interview, the founder of Curves, the health club for women, told me that was the secret to her success as a businesswoman. What a wonderful story of not despising small beginnings! She started with one workout location and now has a nationwide franchise, but her big secret was that she worked within her means until she had more.

So, my friend, it is time to take pen in hand and add up

the cost of your life. How much do you owe in bills? How much does it cost you to eat every week? to go where you go? to do what you do? Add it all up. Cut the unnecessary fat, and decide that's how much you have to work with. Set the boundaries for yourself before they are set for you. See the big picture. See yourself happily being able to meet all of your financial obligations. I believe God does not want us being prisoners to debt. He wants us to be a lender and not a borrower. And that sounds a whole lot more diva-esque to me than hiding from creditors!

DIVA REVELATION

There's this thing called self-gratification that gets us all in trouble. Focusing on what gratifies the flesh most of the time means that larger and more important issues are being ignored. Our desires are like a fire raging out of control. It keeps going where the path is unhindered. This is why firemen dig trenches to set boundaries that cut off the inferno and cause it to die. Again, this is up to you, but consider the devastation of a fire left unchecked. Having your hair on fire is one thing, but your world on fire? It's not a pretty picture. Remember that trenches, better known as boundaries, keep debt from spreading.

WHAT'S A DIVA TO DO?

- Make a list of all of your monthly expenses.

- Decide how much you can realistically allocate to the cost of your life beyond your bills. That would include eating out, gas, clothing, toiletries, etc.

- Total how much you need to have each month in order to meet your obligations. Separate your wants from your needs.

- Allocate what you make accordingly, set your budget for out-of-pocket expenses after you've paid your tithe to God (10 percent) and your bills and put money in savings (10 percent).

- Log on to DaveRamsey.com and invest in his budgeting software. He also has a program for calculating your expenses in case you need some extra help.

7

THE BENEFITS OF
PLASTIC SURGERY

NOW THAT YOU'RE on the road to recovery and have started to use a budget to set your boundaries, let me tell you, the quickest way to blow your budget is to use credit cards. Credit cards are deceptive because they make you think you have more money than you really do. Credit cards are virtual money (kinda like the stock market). Credit cards make you believe you have money until you get the bill. Again, the words of "Ms. Curves" ring true: Never spend money you don't have. The deception of credit cards is that you think you will have the money by the time the bill comes. But usually by then, you've found something else to charge, and the billing cycle continues . . . until you've maxed out your limit. By this point you pay just enough to be able to keep charging within the window you've created for yourself . . . aah, am I singing to the choir here? reading anyone's mail? I thought so.

The thing I hated about my budget was that a major chunk of my money was allocated to paying down credit-card debt. Nothing can be more frustrating than still paying for a suit you've worn so much that you are ready for a new one. It just doesn't seem right. Now one of my friends has a policy that when she charges an outfit, she doesn't wear it until she's paid the bill. But I wonder, *What is the point of doing that?* Why buy an outfit now if you have to hang it in your closet and wait to wear it? She reasons that the exact outfit in her size might not be available by the time she has the money for it, which kind of makes sense, but that doesn't change the fact that I'm not happy about paying for something long after the thrill of acquiring it is gone. Something just doesn't seem right about that . . . and that is the nature of the credit-card cycle!

The deception of credit cards is that you think you will have the money by the time the bill comes. But usually by then, you've found something else to charge, and the billing cycle continues . . . until you've maxed out your limit.

I know I am not the only person who has been caught up in this cycle (creditors thrive off this), but I should know better. I go to Ghana to visit my dad, Mr. Hammond, several times a year. I've always marveled at the cash-and-carry mentality of the society at large. I've had several friends build homes bit by bit; as they got the money, they went to the next step in their building projects. If they didn't have any money, the building stopped. At the end of the day, when they moved into the house, it was completely paid for! Same thing with cars, etc. I was sad the day I saw credit being offered in Ghana; there was something inspiring about seeing people who actually owned everything they had. No wonder the Bible says that you become a slave to the lender.[1] I was working to pay everybody but myself!

So as a part of my financial recovery plan, I had to face the fact that my credit-card bills were not going down because I just kept making room for more purchases. Something had to give, and it wasn't going to be the credit card companies. I made a drastic decision. It was time for plastic surgery. Yup, you got it—time to snip up some of those cards and exercise self-control with the others. Some cards I closed. I kept only the cards that gave me something back, like points that went toward being able to get something for free. (Let's face it, it isn't really free, but it feels like it.) I love my Needless Markup—I mean, my Neiman Marcus—card for that, so I keep it for the end-of-the-season sales and then put it away until the next drastic markdown sale, better known as Last Call. That's when I feel as if I get a present back when all my points from shopping add up and can be redeemed for dollars; yes, girl, it's a beautiful thing!

Nothing can be more frustrating than still paying for a suit you've worn so much that you are ready for a new one.

But back to plastic surgery: As for the few department

store cards I had left, I put them away after I called and had the limits lowered on them. Hey, does an alcoholic leave their favorite libations lying around in full view? I had to set limits for myself. I knew my illness. Lowering the limits ensured that if I had a relapse, I wouldn't be able to do extreme harm to myself. After all, if you don't have your card with you, the store clerks are more than happy to look up your number and give you access to your credit. In the midst of a good sale, that could be dangerous, but not if your limit is low. My new philosophy was if I couldn't pay for it with cash, I probably didn't need it anyway, although for most shopaholics *need* has nothing to do with the equation. Can I get an amen?

Finance gurus say it looks better on your credit score if you have more than half of your limit free on credit cards. My goal was to get to ground zero and then use every card I had as if it were an American Express, which meant I could not purchase more than I could pay for when the bill came. (The traditional American Express card requires that you pay off your balance each month.) Here's the thing you must keep in mind whenever you're tempted to use credit cards: Life happens. The money you don't have now, you may never have. Therefore, you should never play with credit cards based on future earnings. What if you lose your job? What if your car suddenly needs to be fixed? The laundry list of what can and will go wrong is long and a gamble most can't afford to take. What *can* happen usually does.

I do realize you need to have some sort of credit card because the world literally makes it impossible for you not to. You need credit cards for identification, for checking into hotels, for purchasing things online; however, trouble awaits you when you fall into the trap of not keeping up with how much you're spending every time you whip that bad boy out and slap it down on a counter. Before you know it, you are clutching your pearls when you find yourself looking down at the damage done in a month's time. This is when you have to take your life by the reins and drive it. Remember: You are to have the credit card. The credit card should not have you.

If you must use your credit card, keeping a ledger of all your purchases will help you know when to stop. Once again, set your budget. Decide how much you can afford for eating out, magazines, Starbucks, all the stuff you do beyond your household expenses and other bills. Even though you're using your credit card, you have to stay within the boundaries. Keep a little notebook in your purse. Whenever you spend something, whether it is cash, debit, or credit, write it down. That way you will always know how much you have to work with. Mint.com is a great free application to help you keep track of your budget and your expenditures. You enter all your bills and your banking info, and it keeps track of your spending and shows you your balances across the board. It also shows you how much credit you have available on your card. Everything. It's pretty sobering when you can constantly see what you still owe—the total staring you in the face. It's much more fun to watch the numbers go down. It can become a game for you—kinda like when you lose a nice chunk of weight, seeing the scale go down encourages you to keep going.

If all else fails and you find you cannot set boundaries and still use your credit card, get a prepaid PayPal credit card. You can link it to your bank account and transfer money onto it. That way you never spend what you don't have. *And,* you can actually make money while you're spending it! That's right; PayPal pays you one percent back for every dollar you spend *plus* interest on what is sitting in your account. You can't beat that with a stick!

So there you have it: several options at your disposal to help you get a handle on the plastic. To choose the best option, you need to be completely honest with yourself. If you cannot exercise self-control, then close all your cards down and get a prepaid one. That way you can only spend what you already paid for. This may sound drastic, but drastic times call for drastic measures. And nothing that is smaller than you should ever have the power to put you in bondage. It's just so undiva-like!

DIVA REVELATION

In a perfect world, I really think one credit card would be enough. If you own your own business, two cards are fine— one for personal expenses, one for business expenses. This will make your accountant very happy. Try not to use your debit card for purchases; use it only for cash withdrawals. This keeps scam artists from having access to your bank account and makes contesting charges and handling refunds a lot easier. True mastery is when your bank account is used to store your money and pay your bills in full at the end of the month. This is the vision we all need to write and make plain so we can see it come to fruition.

WHAT'S A DIVA TO DO?

- Line up your cards, kiss them good-bye, and put them away!

- Pay down cards and eliminate their use except for emergencies (and only if you will pay the balance in full when billed).

- Check your credit report to see if it is accurate, and clean up any discrepancies.

- Purpose to pay on time or ahead of time at least five dollars over the minimum.

- Get a prepaid PayPal credit card.

- Get some sort of tracking device for your spending. I highly recommend Mint.com.

- Log on to debtproofliving.com and check out their Rapid Debt Repayment Plan.

8

THE POWER OF THE LITTLE ENVELOPE AND LOOSE CHANGE

ONCE UPON A TIME I had a wonderful, large urn that sat in a corner of my room. All of my loose change went into it. It became so heavy that I couldn't move it. Then one day, I had to move it—I was moving (as in moving from one apartment to another). I had to empty my heavy urn out in order to move. After shoveling the coins into several bags so they could be carried, I dragged them to the bank. You would not believe how much those little coins added up to! Over five hundred dollars! See what I mean about not despising small beginnings? Little things add up. It was an eye-opener for me to finally understand this concept in a whole new light.

Just as little things can add up, they can dissipate subtly. This is why I love the concept of the little envelope. Oh alright, you can have *froufrou* envelopes or a little wallet-size accordion file in some hot color just to entertain yourself if you want to. Financial expert Dave Ramsey has a deluxe envelope system all ready for you. He even has a designer version in diva red! Just log on to the online store at daveramsey.com to see all the tools he has available to help you get on track and stay there. Basically, what I want you to do is to live on a cash basis for a week so you can get a grip on exactly how much money you spend per week or even per day. After you've decided the budget for your expenditures, put cash in envelopes and label them. Eating out, carfare, magazines, whatever! Here is where the rubber hits the road, girl. You will be amazed at how thoughtlessly you've thrown around your cards and money before. Now, every time you spend money, you'll see how much you have left to work with. You are going to have to keep yourself honest on this one. When you get to the bottom of your envelope, that's it. You don't get any more until next week (or next month, depending on how often you set your budget). So if you blow your whole stash by Tuesday, no more eating out for you for the rest of the week. Sounds scary, doesn't it? But think of it this way— you could lose some weight!

I'm not saying you have to do this for the rest of your life, but do it long enough to see how you spend your money and learn how to pace yourself. Graduation day would be when you have more money than week left. Get it? I learned this one from my sister, Miss Thrifty to the Highest Degree. That girl can squeeze a nickel and make it weep. She and her husband had all these white envelopes all over the place. She was always calculating how much she could spend to stretch her shekels, as I would call them. I was completely incredulous when I first got wind of this. Now I'm a believer.

I found myself being totally indignant about how quickly my money dwindled. It was as if it grew wings and flew away. More than once I heard myself saying, "Now where did all my money go? I know I had forty dollars in here this morning!" It was amazing to me how much I didn't think about how all of my little purchases added up to one whopping bottom line that cleaned out my account in what seemed to be the blink of an eye. It was more like a thoughtless flick of the wrist! After accepting the horror that all my little expenditures were rapidly becoming a mountain I could no longer climb, my spending became much more earthbound. Okay, so I didn't need to buy three different packets of Orbit gum just because I didn't know which flavor I might feel like having. I had to make a choice and stick to it until it was finished. Hmm, that one revelation bled into a bunch of other areas I will share with you later.

Last but not least, keeping your receipts really is a good thing. This is another way to review all of your expenditures. Collect them and then add them up at the end of the week.

It was amazing to me how much I didn't think about how all of my little purchases added up to one whopping bottom line that cleaned out my account in what seemed to be the blink of an eye.

Those little slips of paper will show you where your heart really is. Trust me, you will be amazed. Again, you'll get a real revelation on your personal idols. Where your treasure is, your heart is also.[1] This may call for some recalibration of the things that are really important. Those little sheets of paper won't lie; they will tell the truth about what you think about the most and what has been doing a good job of consuming your money without you being the wiser.

The way you spend money says more about your heart and your spirit than you know.

Needless to say, if those little white envelopes could talk, they would have some tales to tell. Some we would not like them to repeat, I'm sure. But all in all, if you can stick this exercise out, they will tell of how you learned to work within the safe confines of what you had and came out the richer for it.

DIVA REVELATION

It's been said we perish for lack of knowledge.[2] In the area of finance especially, what you don't know *can* hurt you. It's definitely time to wise up and spend right. The way you spend money says more about your heart and your spirit than you know. As you realign your priorities, you will see shifts in your character as well and find greater wealth than you've ever dreamed. 'Cause one thing you will learn while you're broke is that there is a difference between wealth and riches. A life well lived with spiritual, emotional, and physical good health, along with contentment, is true wealth; riches are the accumulation of trinkets that can come and go and seriously mess with your peace and joy level.

WHAT'S A DIVA TO DO?

- Establish the white envelope rule. All daily living expenses are to be paid for in cash.

- Budget yourself accordingly. You are not allowed to withdraw more money if you run out. What's in your white envelope is all you have to work with.

- Keep a ledger of what you spend and what you purchase. You'll be surprised to see where your money goes and how little purchases add up.

9

HOW TO SAY NO
AND STILL LOOK
BEAUTIFUL

LET'S FACE IT. Sometimes a diva can have eyes that are
bigger than her budget. That's when one needs to make a
quality decision based on criteria other than "I want it." Do
you really *need* it is the question. Of course, I agree with the
concept that you can never have too many white blouses or
black shoes, but the line has to be drawn somewhere—that
somewhere being your wallet.

We live in an instant-gratification world that has cultivated
a nation of spoiled babies. We have ever-available credit,
trends that overwhelm us, and our neighbors, the Joneses, to

keep up with. Naturally, we're left asking, "Why shouldn't I have that?" If you're trying to get ahead in life, image is everything, right? This train of thought, also known as deception, can run up quite a tab. On top of that, add the rationale, "I owe it to myself!" and you find (or lose) yourself charging down the aisles of your favorite store.

Now I don't know about you, but I can certainly find at least one occasion a day to reward myself with some trinket or object of my desire. *I worked hard today, I bumped my toe, I finished a project, I haven't had a break, I'm happy, I'm sad, I lost five pounds, I gained seven*—you name it, I can fashion a reason (pardon the pun) for a retail celebration, or retail therapy is more like it. When I go down this lane of constantly rewarding myself, by the time the bills catch up with me, I need a real therapist. Isn't it amazing how delusional we can be? You get the credit-card statement and have the nerve to be shocked: "How did this bill get so high?" You act as if your card had been abducted by someone who secretly used it and put it back in your wallet. Duh. I've played the nut role before too.

As I said in chapter 6, I'm always fascinated by those who have mastered restraint. As I think about who those people are, it reveals the hidden issue with those who haven't. People who say no are highly disciplined people who may even be seen as selfish, because not only can they say no to a sale, but they can say no to you. They are not people pleasers and don't feel any obligation to take on false burdens or absorb guilt about not cooperating with your plans. They have charted their courses regarding how much time as well as money they have to spend on any given venture and refuse to wander beyond the confines of the choices they've already made for themselves. They usually have a personal program that is established and a set routine and way of doing things. Every move they make is calculated and factored into the bottom line of where they want to end up. To those who are the opposite, these highly disciplined types can seem too regimented and appear not to be having much fun. However, they usually have much more peace and way less drama in their lives.

Those who have a hard time saying no are more of the whimsical, carefree persuasion. If I did a temperament study, I would say the highest on the list of those having a hard time saying no would be those of the sanguine temperament. They want everyone to be happy, including themselves. Unfortunately this usually causes them to overbook and overextend themselves, and they fall in an exhausted heap at the end of the day. Of course, those who can easily say no tend to be more choleric, or doers, because they are more task driven versus people driven.

Caregivers and people pleasers also have a hard time saying no. All of this adds up to having a spirit of entitlement. Ah yes, there it is: You deserve a reward because of how much you give yourself and your time away to others. This becomes the greatest excuse for self-indulgence. This is why it is important to ask yourself what you truly value and what your motivation is for the things that you do—the opinions of others or your personal health and financial security?

We live in an instant-gratification world that has cultivated a nation of spoiled babies. We have ever-available credit, trends that overwhelm us, and our neighbors, the Joneses, to keep up with.

Now just so you people pleasers and caregivers don't walk away feeling too bad about yourselves, remember that people who can say no aren't perfect either; they just find their value in other things. Trust me, they may be saying no to a sale, but they are saying yes to something else that may not interest you. They might say yes to getting bogged down in the details and becoming excessive workaholics because of their natures driven to master everything. We all have that "one thing" that we wrestle with. It may not be costing them financially, but it could be costing them in other ways. But, back to you.

Consider the benefits of saying no. Think about the bottom line and what saying no will save you from. Debt. Frustration. Resentment. Regret. Saying no to some indulgences and to some people will help you be your best for the times you do say yes to *some* things and to those you love; saying no will also reveal the very real truth that there is power in realizing that you cannot be all things to all people, and that is alright. For every time that you say no, you leave room for someone else to rise to the occasion. You might be blocking someone else's growth and development because you are enabling them to continue doing nothing. Oooh! I just heard some toes go *crunch*. The reality is that, if you don't do it, someone else will. The world will not fall off its axis. Life will go on. That whole superwoman thing is really a minigod complex. The only person who can be God is God; others have tried and failed miserably—don't even go there.

Likewise, you cannot own absolutely everything. Leave something for someone else to have a gander at, why don't ya? Saying no is actually a beauty secret. It works the lip muscles and does wonders for highlighting the cheekbones. If you say yes too often, it could create lines on either side of the mouth, as well as worry lines from all the debt you incur. So go ahead, purse those beautiful diva lips and practice saying it: "No . . . no . . . no!" There, don't you feel empowered?

DIVA REVELATION

Not being able to say no is grounded in fear and pride. Neither is healthy. Either you believe that every good and perfect gift is yours at the right time or you don't.[1] As they say, "The world can't take away what the good Lord gives you," but if you decide to do all the hoarding yourself, you will wear yourself out trying to keep what you gathered. Just remember, for every good sale that you miss, there will be another one with better stuff—you can bank on it.

Saying no to some indulgences and to some people will help you be your best for the times you do say yes to some things and to those you love.

WHAT'S A DIVA TO DO?

- Declare a shopping fast for a month.

- Don't buy anything you don't absolutely need or have not run out of.

- Keep a list of every time you break this rule.

- For every purchase you make that is not a must-have item, you must give something away.

10

A WOMAN'S GOT TO HAVE PRIORITIES

ONE OF THE easiest ways to master saying no without feeling guilt, shame, or like you're missing out on something is to have your priorities straight. You have to decide what is more important to you—being debt free or being fabulous on the surface while your internal world is a hot mess from the stress you've created for yourself. There is this little thing in life called leverage. Leverage is the thing that propels you in another direction. It can literally unearth you from where you had planted yourself and put you on another path based on the urgency of what you need or desire most.

When I first moved into my new home, my priorities changed. My focus went from making *me* look beautiful to making my *home* look beautiful. I would find myself standing in the aisle of a store, going, "Dress, doorknobs, dress, doorknobs . . ." The doorknobs won because I wanted to finish my home. The same has to apply across the board with everything in your life. It's called focus. A house divided against itself cannot stand. It will implode and take your finances and peace of mind with it.

So, my sister, what is more important to you? Being debt-free fabulous from the inside out or perpetrating an image that will cost you more than it's worth in the end? Ah yes, one must stop to consider what does it profit a woman to gain the world, or perhaps just a slamming wardrobe and associated material possessions, and lose her soul *and* her mind. Perhaps part of the problem with having the right priorities has to do with having the right heart condition. The right heart condition will definitely recalibrate your thinking, and once your mind is renewed, you can expect your life to be transformed. I've often said that the definition for insanity is continually doing the same thing and expecting different results. But I also know that habits won't change if minds don't change first. This is why dieting does not work. The fat person inside just resents what the skinny person outside is forcing it to eat. Until your mind and your heart agree that you love eating differently, the fight will continue and the pounds will return. I'm a witness. The same is true with money. It is interesting that the Bible talks so much about money—not the way many preachers do—but the Word certainly reveals what

God's mind-set is toward it. God wants you to have everything you need. He is not against abundance at all. He is against our fixation on money because He knows that opens up a Pandora's box of other issues. "The love of money is the root of all evil."[1] The *love* of it, not the money itself.

First of all, if you make money your pursuit, you will never have enough. The truth of the matter is that you serve what you love. If you make money your lover, you will be consumed with how to get more of it and end up feeling the poorer for it. You can't serve God and money at the same time because you will love one and hate the other.[2] Why? Because serving money can drive you to make choices that would not please God at all. Money should never be the boss of you.

The right heart condition will definitely recalibrate your thinking, and once your mind is renewed, you can expect your life to be transformed.

So many have fallen into the trap of building kingdoms they don't have the money to pay for. The added stress and strain of trying to feed the demands of the life you've created or the venture you've begun can kill the joy you thought you would get from what you've acquired. This is not God's design for anyone's life. He promises that His yoke is easy and His burden is light.[3] Based on that one statement, a diva has to stop and assess if she has taken on more than she should have when she finds herself struggling under the burden of her obligations. God forbid you find yourself pushed over the edge into dishonesty or doing things solely for the motivation of how much it will pay in order to stay afloat. Are you doing what you're doing because you feel called and created to do it or because you need the money? Are you doing it out of love and passion or out of desperate need to pay the bills? You can collect all the money in the world and still feel exhausted and empty—even when you're doing good things!

Mm-hmm, if the devil can't make you bad, he will just make you busy. You can be so busy doing all the right things that it can end up being to your detriment, leaving you in a state of poverty—emotionally, spiritually, and relationally. Now don't get me wrong; God has nothing against money. He promises to give you the power to get wealth, but His idea of wealth goes beyond the abundance of money and acquisitions. God wants you to prosper above all things, but He wants you to do it with balance. He wants you to prosper and be in good health even as your *soul* prospers.[4] When your soul is full, you won't feel the need to fill up on other things that work against you. A healthy spirit promotes health and well-being on every level of your life. I think God's idea of wealth is having a life well lived, being wealthy on all fronts so that you are not just full, but satisfied because you feel no lack in any area of your life. That is the diva-licious life!

You can collect all the money in the world and still feel exhausted and empty—even when you're doing good things!

As we purpose to have money and things and not allow them to have us, we have to determine what our true treasure is. I believe it is being of sound mind, body, and soul. I believe that we are all tri-level beings, meaning that we are a soul that has a spirit that lives in a body. You can't ignore any part of yourself (mind, body, or soul) when dealing with any area of life, including money; otherwise, you are out of balance. Being connected to the One who gives all things is paramount. As we take on God's perspective of money, we see that money is something He gives not just for us to bless ourselves but for us to bless others. Again, He wants us to be lenders, not borrowers. He wants us to be empowered by money, not slaves to it. Think about it. All the people who commit crimes of robbery are slaves—slaves to their desire for more without the ability to get it the right way. They are driven to do things that might cost them more if they get caught, but their will is held captive by their desires, so they take the risk. You might not be sticking anybody up, but if you're robbing Peter to pay Paul, in a sense you are a robber too. And the person being robbed is you!

So here we go. Your first and greatest priority has to be sound spiritual grounding. Some call it finding your center. I call it being clear on who you are and Whose you are. If you know you are a child of God, all of your other decisions will be made based on that knowledge. It's trusting that all your needs will be supplied so you don't walk in desperation. It's also owning the fact that you've been entrusted to be a good steward of what God has given you. If you gave someone a million dollars and they blew it all on material items for themselves, would you want to give them more? No, you wouldn't. But if you saw them handling what you had given them responsibly, investing it wisely and blessing others with it, you would want to give them more.

My sister has a rule at her house that I admire. She will

not buy an item that is a want unless she can match the amount spent on a charitable venture. This blew me away; it's a wonderful way to set boundaries that keep them from being wasteful. This rule keeps them from buying things just because they can. This is a covenant she's made to keep herself spiritually grounded. I must admit I'm still working on this one, but the thought is ever present in the back of my mind, and it has slowed me down a tad. My friend Holly always asks when we're out shopping and I start to linger over something, "Is it a need or a greed?" Good question.

On the flip side, you may be like another friend, who just told me, "But, Michelle, I'm generous; as a matter of fact, I give most of my money away, and that's why I don't have any. I'm always helping other people out." Sometimes you can be generous to a fault. I've been guilty of this—helping and rescuing others because somewhere inside of me was that minigod thing. Helping and rescuing others made me important, indispensable, and loved . . . or so I thought. Until one day it occurred to me that perhaps I gave in order to be loved. In my eyes, I wasn't lovable unless I was always playing the hero. How sick is that? I had to examine my motivations. If I found any expectation associated with my giving, I decided I would not. I wanted pure relationships more than codependency. After all, even God doesn't force us to love Him. He doesn't bribe and cajole us into becoming His ardent followers. His generosity is solely based on His love for us, no strings attached. If we choose to respond to Him, we are the richer for it. We must have a higher priority than the acquisition of things in order to be free. Your heart will follow after whatever you treasure and leave you bank-rupt if your priorities are not in the right place. And that, my friends, does not look pretty in any diva's portfolio.

DIVA REVELATION

Priorities are the true measurement of your maturity. Chil-dren's eyes will always be bigger than their stomachs or their incomes. As we mature, it's time to put away childish things and make more responsible decisions. As we survey the landscape of life, knowing that nothing is permanent and tomorrow is not promised, we must walk circumspectly, understanding the times and being sensitive to the changes they imply. We must count the cost of our decisions before we have to pay for them and pursue peace at all costs. That is the foundation of independence—that we are not left want-ing or owing.

WHAT'S A DIVA TO DO?

- Write down all the things you've spent money on in the past month—I mean everything from that cup of Starbucks to that extra pack of gum and the magazine.

- Separate your wants from your needs.

- Now number them in order of importance.

- Put a line through the things that are robbers of your cash flow.

11

THE FRUIT OF
LIVING GENEROUSLY

THERE IS SOMETHING to be said for planting or investing seed in good ground and getting a return for it. Sometimes you don't see that return for quite a while. As a matter of fact, most of the time you don't see a return from the same source to which you've given. Therefore you should never have a "you owe me" attitude when you give to folk. The root travels, and you don't know where it will end up. I make it a personal policy never to loan people what I can't afford to give away. It just makes life easier and keeps offense at an all-time low. Giving to receive is a major setup for disappointment. To give freely is a reward in itself. Every time I give something to someone, I rejoice in the fact that I had it to give—it is true that it is better to give than to receive. Ultimately it is God who is our banker. He observes our giving and pays us according to our willingness to give through strangers, friends, or the work of our hands. It's best to leave the source up to Him.

I remember when we borrowed money from one another in school, we would always say, "As long as you owe me, I'll never be broke." This is true to a great degree. It was understood that we knew we could always count on one another should a real need arise. When I fell on hard times, it was amazing how living generously paid dividends back to me before I even let my friends know what was happening.

During my time of financial struggle, eating out and indulging my idiosyncrasies fell by the wayside for sure. Milan and Matisse, my two shih tzus, were eating better than I was as I watched my pennies. It was amazing how people started coming out of the woodwork, offering to take me to dinner—just because. I wondered if a secret memo had been distributed among them, but a lot of them had no connection to one another. *It had to be divine intervention,* I concluded. For everyone to suddenly be on a whim to take Michelle to dinner could be no accident. Some were people I had helped out when they'd gone through difficult times, but some were not. It all seemed rather serendipitous, but I knew better. All I could do was thank them and mutter, "Thank you, God," under my breath. This divine provision covered everything extending past free dinners to other things that might seem insignificant to some but were important to me.

Just as I was bemoaning running out of my favorite bath gel, another friend who had stayed at my house for a while when she'd been in transition just happened to pick me up a bottle. When I exclaimed in glee over my gift, she just shrugged and said, "Well, you're always getting me things, so I decided to pick you up something I knew you liked!" I was humbled.

Giving to receive is a major setup for disappointment.

Trust me, nothing humbles you like receiving when you are the one who is used to giving, and yet it is just as important to learn how to receive graciously as it is to learn to give generously. What you pour out will always come back to you in greater measure than what you gave. Whatever you want to receive, you must give first. Love, things, money—you name it, it is guaranteed to overtake you if you give freely without looking for a return. A generous heart generates favor and invites unlimited gifts into your life. This is why even when you have very little, you must resist the tendency to hoard what you have. This is the quickest way to run out of the little you are trying to hold on to. Ah, but when you share what you have with others (with no ulterior motives), no matter how little it may appear to be, it will increase before your eyes. I believe that God smiles when we choose to be cheerful givers,[1] and He honors that giving by making sure our coffers are refilled so that we can give again.

This is also why I believe in tithing—giving your first 10 percent of increase or earnings to God. You can argue about if you should give the net or the gross of your income all day long if you want to. I simply ask, "Do you want the net or the gross of what God has for you?" Stingy begets stingy. Generous begets overflow. Tithing may be one of the hardest battles you will ever fight because, again, it reveals who you serve and what really rules your heart. When money is your master, you serve a hard taskmaster who promises you nothing but grief and aggravation. But when God is the master of your heart, you rest in His ability to provide for you and protect what you have. Here is the caveat, and mind you, it's my personal opinion. Without getting into a deep theological debate, I believe that God promises to keep the "devourer" from robbing you if you tithe. If you don't tithe, He calls it robbery. One robbery leaves you open for another. You can read it for yourself in Malachi 3:8-12. Based on this, I don't think God has to protect your stuff if you don't sign up for His insurance policy. I see the tithe as your insurance. What happens when you allow your insurance with Allstate to expire? You find you are no longer in "good hands."

A generous heart generates favor and invites unlimited gifts into your life.

I think you can't afford *not* to tithe. I find that whenever I don't tithe, my money gets funny, and when I do, no matter how little I have, it stretches beyond my expectations and all my needs are covered. God promises to protect you from being robbed if you invest in His Kingdom by giving Him your "firstfruits." He really could ask for more, since He gives you the ability to gain wealth in the first place. He asks for less than Uncle Sam! It's not because God needs your money; it really is about checking out where your heart really is and having you help others who are in need. A surrendered heart is not ruled by the flesh and all the things it insists on having. It is God's way of reining us in and keeping us and all we have safe. When we tithe and give our offerings in this light, we are able to give joyously.

I remember when I was unemployed many years ago. I was sad because I didn't have a lot to give, but I gave the first 10 percent of my unemployment check. And like the story about the five loaves of bread and two fish that Jesus used to feed five thousand people, I can honestly say that I saw my resources stretch to cover my needs and I did not suffer lack![2] It was a miracle. When I finally did run out of money, a lady offered me a place to stay for free! Now you know that is a miracle. And there I stayed until a month later I was blessed with a wonderful job and a whopping raise that made all the struggle worthwhile. He gives seed to the sower.[3]

What exactly does that look like? Well, consider when you take a seed and put it in the ground; it grows and creates something that can be profitable to the one who harvests it. The seed creates food that the farmer sells for a profit, that someone else eats. . . . You see where I'm going with this? God gives us the ability to provide for ourselves and others— it's the law of sowing and reaping. Yes, my friend, you will reap whatever you sow—financially, relationally, across the board. This is the cycle of life. When we embrace it, we prosper on all levels, and that sounds like a good deal to me!

DIVA REVELATION

In a sense, all the money you have is basically on loan from God to you, which means He should be able to ask you for as much of it as He wants, and yet He does not abuse that privilege. This may sound a little black-and-white to you, and that's because it is. If God doesn't have free access to your money, He doesn't have free access to you. Plain and simple. I think that if God doesn't have access to you, He is not obligated to look out for you and all concerning you. Choosing a relationship with your money, which will always be one sided, versus a relationship with God, is a losing proposition. A relationship with God gives you access to all He has. As long as what is yours is His, then what is His is yours; and trust me, sister, He has way more stuff and resources than you do!

WHAT'S A DIVA TO DO?

- Revamp the proportion of your spending—10 percent to God, 10 percent to savings, 80 percent to living. If you are brave, set aside an additional 10 percent for investments apart from savings.

- Invest in a cause that is important to God. This will always pay dividends. (I've adopted four World Vision children that I support monthly.)

- Make sure you save something. The rule used to be that you should have enough to cover six months of your expenses. The newer reports recommend one year's worth! However, don't let your focus on saving make you tightfisted. Don't be driven by fear to stop being generous to those in need. When the needs of others are a priority in your life, you will always miraculously have what you need. (The operative word here being *need*!)

12

THE POWER OF
A SOCIAL LIFE

I FIND THAT there are two poles or extremes when it comes to
how people interact. There are those who pride themselves on
being independent, and then there are those who pride themselves on being master networkers. Networkers are passionate
about networking. They believe that networking is the secret
to success. Relationships, whether nurtured on the golf course
or during after-work gatherings, form bonds that increase your
chances of success in the arena where you interact.

It is true, relationships are important. We were created for
relationship. Part of living a fabulous life has to do with being

well connected—that is, thriving in healthy relationships with God, yourself, family, friends, significant others, and those you encounter every day. Healthy and fruitful relationships are crucial to your well-being. Why? Because when people don't like you or feel comfortable around you, they don't help you. And that can really hurt you. When people like you, they will assist you on your journey and make the path to success a lot easier. This is why people love organizations, fraternities, sororities, clubs, etc. They supply support.

Though many pride themselves on being independent, let me tell you that independence is highly overrated and can set you up for being isolated at times when having the right associations could be critical to your existence. We were not made for independence; we were made to interact with, sustain, and maintain one another. You will never know how much your little toe plays into your balance until you lose it. That is why all of the parts of the body are needed and no part is insignificant, just like no person is insignificant. In theater, they say there are no small parts—only small actors.

Healthy and fruitful relationships are crucial to your well-being.

I remember when, years ago, the garbagemen went on strike. That was when they won people's respect. No one had ever thought about what would happen if someone didn't dispose of garbage. It could literally affect the world as disease began to spread from the remains . . . ew, just the thought of it is horrible! But hopefully the point is well taken that we all need one another doing what each one of us does to function well and not lose ground in this journey we call life.

Now this is just my personal opinion, but I truly believe that God has actually allowed us to come to this place financially as a nation because we need to get back to basics. We need to get back to a sense of community, sharing and bearing one another's burdens. I heard someone say the other day, "Hey, you just need to be nice to everyone these days. Who knows? You may end up having to live with them!" I also find it interesting that during the recession, the divorce rate has dipped. People can't afford to get divorces, so they have to stay and work it out. I say amen to that!

During times of plenty, we sometimes gave in to the "easy" way of resolving problems; our larger bank accounts could handle a few more hits, so why work things out? Why put up with anything that made us uncomfortable? We could afford to walk away. We had better relationships with our computers, Facebook, and Twitter, which gave us far too many other ways to hide from working through our immediate relationships and nurturing intimacy. In times of plenty, we were able to avoid transparency and accountability, and we became one selfish, self-absorbed society. We were all so independent that we were having long-distance relationships in our homes. So along comes a financial whirlwind to shake up our world and pare down all our precious distractions, and what do we have left at the end of the day? That's right—relationships. All we have left are the folk who love us. There's nothing like need to bring us back to ground zero.

Another way to look at the need for viable relationships is through the concept of circulation. Circulating is key. There is a reason the Dead Sea is called the Dead Sea; it has no outlet, so its water remains stagnant. Likewise, when we are not mixing and mingling, sharing common interests, we die and lose opportunities to meet others who can introduce us to others who might lead us to the very door we need to enter to gain access to provision, dreams, or perhaps just a dream man. With the exception of those who meet on the Internet, most people who marry are introduced by mutual friends—other people they both knew—and discover each other by circulating within their networks. In business the same philosophy holds true. Relationships are, more often than not, the greatest factor in closing deals.

How does circulation translate in financially stressful times? It's simple, but true: Your relationships can carry you through this financial crisis. Sharing knowledge, resources, support . . . there is no room for pride. For those who have lost everything, they already know that there is nothing left to lose. When you are no longer married to anything—your pride, your possessions, your image—you're open to gain more than what you had before. So don't stop getting out there. Rub elbows. Share stories. Again, you'll be surprised to find out how many others are in exactly the same boat as you; and that's when it can get exciting as you share ideas and anecdotes that not only strengthen you but give you tools for moving forward. And finally, if you still need proof to get out there and circulate, remember, we all know that when it comes to seeing and being seen, no one does that better than a diva!

We were not made for independence; we were made to interact with, sustain, and maintain one another.

DIVA REVELATION

Never have a relationship based only on what you can get from the exchange. Never make money or opportunity part of the equation. Delight in authentically enjoying the associations you have been afforded, and let them bear their own fruit. That way no one feels used, and at the end of the day, if nothing material comes out of the relationship, you are still richer in some other dimension for the time you've shared. Relationships are your hidden wealth—invest in them; this is stock that never goes down and always matures with time.

WHAT'S A DIVA TO DO?

- Take stock of your friendships.

- Clarify what you gain from each one.

- Take note of what you have to offer to each one.

- Strive for quality over quantity of time spent.

- Make a date to nurture a relationship you've over-looked for a time and reengage.

13

THE SECRET OF COMMUNITY

I WAS RECENTLY in a cab on the way to the airport, and my cabdriver told me a wonderful story about community. One family in his neighborhood had a home in foreclosure. Several of their neighbors formed a committee and asked the family what they needed to save their home. You see, the neighbors didn't want the house to be taken by the bank, because they realized that all of their property values would go down if a home in the neighborhood were sold at a lower price. If only we could all see life through this lens. When one person loses, we all lose.

Perhaps that is the philosophy of the early church when the Bible points out in the book of Acts that the new converts sold everything they had and shared all things in common so that every need was met.[1] I am not suggesting that we go back to communal living, but I am seriously advocating walking in community. Are you your brother's or sister's keeper? The answer is yes, you'd better be, because if you are not, there will be a price to pay for it somewhere along the way! Call it the domino effect. All I know is that, when the economy sneezes, everyone eventually gets a cold. No one is exempt from the effects. It behooves us to have a mind-set that is open to sharing and doing what can be done to help a sistah or a brotha out.

Within my circle of friends, we meet regularly to find out what the needs are in our group. We've been doing this for over twenty years. And yes, we have passed the plate around several times. We've joked about purchasing a house and getting all the single women to live together. Hey! Drastic times call for drastic measures! It's time-out for "what's mine is mine and what's yours is yours." Now it's share and share alike if you are going to make it.

When one person loses, we all lose.

The word *community* suggests that you have things in common. Community suggests that you have things that you share—not just words, but help, resources, wisdom, or whatever is needed. Community is a place to be transparent and take the hard sayings along with the comforting ones. It's the place where you pool what you have to shore up the one in need, understanding that times and seasons change and the next time it could be you standing in the place of need. Common, commune, community. It is an entity where all things in common are shared while we commune together. It is your extended family, and everyone should have one. They say you can't pick your family, but you can pick your friends.

My church has a program called TheCommon.org. Anyone who is a member of the church can enter the skills and resources they have into a data bank in the lobby. Those who have a need also enter their requests into the data bank. The needs and requests can range from needing a dogsitter, needing your house painted, needing furniture, a realtor, credit counselor . . . whatever it is you might need. Those in need are matched with those who can supply that need. It's a beautiful thing. It creates a family atmosphere with everyone looking out for one another.

Another example of community is when a group of my friends signed up for the family plan and then split the phone bill to save money. Clever! There is nothing like trial to solidify bonds between people. Those who are able to weather storms together usually come out a lot more dedicated to one another than those who don't go through anything. Developing a family frame of mind ensures that you have a built-in support system for bearing one another's burdens as well as for sharing the load.

Community is a place to be transparent and take the hard sayings along with the comforting ones.

Relationships require time and sacrifice. It is the investments you make into those in your circle that reap great dividends for you in the end. You can sow into good ground or bad ground. What you pour into will either give you more than you put in or rob you blind. It's called investing. If you put your money on a stock that everyone has said is losing value, you can't complain when you see no return from it. So consider your friends carefully. It's not about what you can get out of them, but are they people rich in things that are beneficial to your life so that when you give to them, you feel as if you are making a wise choice? You should be richer for knowing the people that you know. If they are emotional and financial drains, those relationships are not a wise way to spend your time or yourself. I ask myself often if my interactions are promoting my destiny or simply distractions planted to get me offtrack and make me miss my blessing. The older I get, the less time I have to waste on unfruitful ventures as well as detrimental relationships.

We all need one another, and it only takes a succession of crises to make you figure that one out. So why wait until then? What you invest into others today, someone will invest into you. What you withhold, you will find yourself needing somewhere down the line. As we realize that we are all a part of a huge, connected body, we should resist the temptation to isolate ourselves, especially in times of trouble when truly you can find strength in numbers. Decide to actively pursue developing a support system among your inner circle. (Remember the power of circulating from the previous chapter?)

Keep in mind, that doesn't mean living in community will be an easy thing to accomplish. Unity rarely is. As long as there are humans in the mix, there will be conflict. But what relationships do over time is mature and become a place of safety, if you are really willing to do the work. Then when the hard times come, your hair is not on fire because you know you're not alone. And that, my friend, is truly rich!

DIVA REVELATION

We were created for community. When we avoid it, we are pressed into situations that require it. Not only do you need others, but others need you! Everyone searches for significance in this world. People love to help people. Go ahead and give them the opportunity. Dare to be transparent about your needs, and watch people rise to the occasion. Remember that life is a two-way street. As you search for ways to add to the lives of others, you will find all that you give out coming back to you above and beyond the measure of your initial investment. Don't keep track of what you give, but do notice when God blesses you. Love generously, share yourself and all you have openly, and give with abandon. Don't fret, my pet, it always comes back—in abundant measures of love as well as tangible things. Remember, a life rich in relationships is the most lavish existence you will ever experience.

WHAT'S A DIVA TO DO?

- Gather your inner circle together. Discuss what your needs are and how you can support one another.

- Create your own common-need data bank.

- Make sure you set boundaries you all agree on.

14

COSTCO, SAM, AND OTHER FAMOUS FRIENDS

I FOUND THAT a big step toward my financial recovery was not only to look at what I had been spending my money on (remember our idols from chapter 4), but also to look at where I was spending my money. For instance, grocery and neighborhood stores are convenient, but they also tend to be pricey; and if you're anything like me, at the end of the day, you end up throwing away more than you use. This is where that community we discussed in the previous chapter kicks in big time. Form a shopping club. Wait a minute, don't get too happy, because we're not talking shopping for shoes here; we're talking groceries and basic essentials.

A shopping club is one place where you can share and not be mad afterwards. And the shopping club can turn out to be a lot of fun. It's a great reason to get together, have fun, and accomplish a much-needed task, namely that of saving money! You pick the day and time, round up the troops, and go forth ready to conquer. Sometimes you have to swerve off the mainstream to discover hidden treasures.

Costco, Sam's Club, Aldi, and stores where you can buy in bulk can be a diva's haven—especially when shared with a friend. There is a reason these places are always full. You name it, every bargain has five more containers than you need or could ever consume. So why not round up your friends, write your lists, and co-op shop? That means you buy the bulk items and break them down to share when you get home, thereby splitting the bill on discount shopping! Trust me, the same rush you felt when you found that blouse at 80 percent off can be felt when you tally up everything you saved as you peruse your haul.

When shopping at these "warehouses," don't just stick to the packaged stuff; check out the fresh stuff. Buy some of those semi-prepared meals and some Glad containers, divvy up the bounty, and eat well at way less money than if you bought the ingredients to prepare it yourself. You can plan out an entire menu this way and have just enough for great meals with no food left to spoil. This is especially great for single women. If you're married, one container may feed your family and again save you way more than if you bought the individual fixin's. I am a believer in home cooking, especially if you have a family. However, we're talking about significant savings, and this is a delicious alternative.

For short runs and smaller amounts of fresh foods, make sure you're shopping where you have a savings card. I always do a little dance when I see how much I've saved after having them swipe my card. You may also find some great prices at wholesale fresh markets and the farmers' market during the summer. This can be a whole new experience in itself. I find myself eating healthier and losing weight, not because of poverty but because I am more exposed to fresh choices. I'm trying out vegetables and fruits that are not at my major grocery stores, and because fruits and vegetables are the focus of these fresh markets, the produce seems to be in fresher supply, which means they are more delicious. Since they are more delicious, I eat more of them and crave junk less. It's all good. As I streamline my diet to fit my budget, my expenses are not the only thing getting slimmer . . . and that is a beautiful thing.

If you're the type that can't control yourself when you go to the grocery store, shopping online at Peapod (or a similar home delivery service) might be a better idea for you. This will help you stick to your list. Log on, type in what you're looking for, and they'll give you a list of choices; you pick what you want, and they deliver it to your door, saving you from losing it in a grocery aisle. Your local store may also have an option where you can order your food online and pick it up or have it delivered to you. These options might be good for you—compare what the cost of an out-of-control spree at the grocery store could cost you versus staying focused and out of temptation's way! Don't forget to check out the coupons offered online and the specials of the week; your menu just might change to fit the sale.

I used to be faithful to Whole Foods, but now I am having an affair with Trader Joe's—as in the grocery store. What a man! If you must shop alone or you are the only cook in your circle of friends, Trader Joe's is perfect for economical, little prepackaged goodies that are simple to pop into the oven. Delicious and nutritious. Their Korean short ribs are my favorite! I just heat them up and add a salad on the side. They also have a great crab-stuffed salmon that is soooo yummy. You can eat rich for under five dollars. We're talking everything from sushi to little French onion soups . . . mighty fine dining. Food does not have to be expensive to taste good. And though you might have gotten used to specific name brands, these options are equally, if not more, delicious. I don't know about you, but my food tastes a whole lot better if I'm not worrying about what I just paid for it.

As I streamline my diet to fit my budget, my expenses are not the only thing getting slimmer . . . and that is a beautiful thing.

And just in case you're not convinced that shopping in the right (bargain) places can pay off, think about what happened to me one day. I was sashaying down the aisles at Trader Joe's when I met this really cute man who was racking up quite a collection of Italian fruit spritzers. They looked pretty yummy. We had a short discussion about them as he tried to convince me to try one. But I was bent on checking out since I was in a hurry. Unfortunately all of my rushing made me forget to get my parking validated. (Did I mention that Joe lets you park for free?) When I ran back into the store to get my ticket validated, I ran into the cute man, who was now checking out. He handed me a spritzer and said, "Please try one on me." Could a woman ask for anything more? Good food, low prices, cute men giving you freebies? There's something to be said for this thing some call "slumming"!

DIVA REVELATION

Sometimes you get what you pay for; sometimes you don't! Food is a necessity, so it would go on the list of priorities, but consider your shopping source for this priority. Now is not the time to be fancy. It's called getting back to basics. This might be a good time to assess your diet; perhaps some of your more expensive habits can be curtailed and put on a list of indulgences for fewer and more special occasions. It's time to get mean and lean on every front, and that makes it a good time to get back to eating the right things. Remember, empty calories make you get hungry faster, which means you eat more. While the right things—lean meats, vegetables, grains, things rich in fiber—keep you full longer and make you eat less. When it comes to eating right and staying on a budget, it's apples to oranges, or should I say, pennies to the dime.

Food is a necessity, so it would go on the list of priorities, but consider your shopping source for this priority.

WHAT'S A DIVA TO DO?

- First clean out your pantry and take stock of what you already have.

- Plan your menu before going to the store and know what you need ahead of time to help you stay focused.

- Form a savings co-op, make your list, check it twice, and get your shop on!

15

ASK AND YOU SHALL RECEIVE, BUT BARTERING IS EVEN BETTER

ONE OF MY fondest memories is that of shopping with Auntie Abba in Ghana, West Africa. Between my auntie Abba and my cousin Joyce, those sisters drove a mean bargain. Now here I am, the little Americanized girl shopping for souvenirs to bring back as proof of my trip to those who couldn't believe I was really going. The marketplace in Ghana is alive with merchants reveling in the entertainment of bargaining. I have never seen anything like it in America, but boy, did I learn a lot!

Before we left to go to the marketplace, Auntie Abba instructed me on how this all worked. If I saw something

I liked, I was to express mild interest, nothing more. The more excited you looked about the item, the harder it would be to get a good price, she warned. Instead, I was to indicate to her what I wanted, and she would go in for the kill (literally—I decided after watching her at work). Off we went to the market.

The first stop was a collection of beautiful little hand-carved boxes that made me want to squeal in delight, but I contained myself. Picking one up and turning it over, I let out a little "hmm" and put it back down. The merchant dove in. "Do you like it, madam?" I hunched my shoulders slightly and sighed. He touched my arm, waving the box in front of my face. "How much you give me?" "Oh, I'm not sure I want it. . . ." I evasively sighed again. Auntie Abba said, "What is the price?" The merchant named his price, to which my aunt threw back her head and replied, "Hah! Are you trying to rob us?!" Then she grabbed my arm, pulled me away from the merchant, and said, "Let's go!" This prompted a rapid-fire negotiation of how much we were willing to give versus how much the merchant was willing to take. Mind you, this type of thing could take anywhere from ten minutes to an hour, depending on how entertained they both were. I stood idly by, now a third party, as they duked it out in Fanti, one of the native languages; every now and then I was able to make out a phrase such as "Oh, get away" and "I don't want trouble." Finally a price was agreed upon, although the merchant didn't look very happy. As we walked away, my aunt laughed after we got out of earshot. "Hah! We robbed him." I felt sorry for the man; I would have buckled at the first round, but not my aunt. She took special pride in getting a good bargain.

Fast-forward to New York City, where my cousin Joyce resided at the time. We were strolling down a street off Fifth Avenue when I spotted the most divine little diamond cross in a window. Inside we dove to inquire about the price. The answer from the salesman deflated me instantly, but not Joyce. She dove into the fray with gusto. Pulling herself up to her full height, she looked at the man and quietly said, "Oh, that is way too much. What is your last price?" I looked at her in shock. I opened my mouth to say, "Chile, we are not in Ghana!" But a look from her silenced me, and to my amazement, the salesclerk said, "Let me ask the manager. I will be right back."

As he scooted off toward the back of the store, the cross tenderly resting in his palm, Joyce turned to me and said, "Never pay the first price. You should know better than that. Always ask them what their last price is, and don't settle for that if it's not what you want to hear." You could have knocked me over with a feather. An hour and a half later and after walking out of the store twice, I walked away with my cross at a quarter of the price he had asked for in the beginning, along with a small crystal Lalique angel sculpture for free! Anyone watching from the outside would have thought a lover's quarrel was going on as the clerk followed me out of the store, begging and pleading and leading me back in. We were fast friends by the time I left, with him kissing me on both cheeks and asking me to come back soon.

Who'da thunk it?! Needless to say, I've now become the

diva of bargaining whenever I can. You would be amazed at what you can walk away with if you only ask! There's something to that Scripture that says, "Ask and you shall receive!"[1] It makes you realize that merchants get away with whatever they can unless you call them on it. I am now quite happy sailing through life, asking for discounts wherever I go. I've walked out of grocery stores with free food because the expiration date was set to kick in within two days of my purchase. I've gotten everything from an extra 10 percent off for a missing button to an additional discount because I was buying more than one thing. All you have to do is ask!

You would be amazed at what you can walk away with if you only ask!

Another absolutely delightful way to get the things you want without spending money is the art of the barter. Service for service or item for item. You've got to make whatever you have (or whatever you can do) work for you. It's called tapping into the hidden economy of your abilities or available resources. Everything is not about money. Sometimes it's an exchange of skill sets. Yes, it's true! People will give you things in exchange for services. After all, everything costs money, and if you don't have to pay for something and you still get something you need, you can call it even. It can be anything. If you paint my place, I'll watch your dog. My girlfriend Pamela does all her aunt's personal shopping in exchange for groceries and cooked meals delivered to her home. I've done writing and design projects in exchange for curtains being made for my home; my seamstress needed a brochure she didn't have money to pay for, and I needed curtains I couldn't afford to have made. We both got what we wanted without spending a dime! Are you getting the picture? There is more than one way to get what you want out of life.

At the center of all of this is a sense of community and building relationships that are open to untraditional modes of giving and taking. (We just can't get away from this concept!) Giving and taking can only be realized in fruitful ways when both people have a sense of the blessing that comes from sharing and pouring into one another's lives. Someone once said the best things in life are free, and perhaps that's true. But the best feeling in life is when you've acquired something you wanted or needed, and you're not the poorer for it.

DIVA REVELATION

Though there is a cost for everything, it doesn't always have to cost what you thought. Sometimes you can get more than you pay for, depending on how much you are willing to engage with others to gain what you want. You have to remember that stores mark up things anywhere from 100 to 500 percent, depending on what is being sold. So remember: There is always room for negotiation.

Everything is not about money. Sometimes it's an exchange of skill sets.

WHAT'S A DIVA TO DO?

- Do your homework. Investigate prices and comparison shop before purchasing pricey items.

- Opt for wholesale opportunities whenever possible.

- Always ask for the last price.

- Log on to swaptree.com to swap items you no longer want or need with someone who has something you're looking for. Call it an even exchange with no fuss, *and* at no expense to you!

16

PUTTIN' ON THE RITZ AND OTHER CREATIVE OPTIONS

I HAVE TO CONFESS that more than eating food, cooking and serving my friends food, or talking over food, I love to eat out. With my financial recovery plan, I now had a dilemma. I had champagne taste but a Kool-Aid budget. When I really decided to crack down, I thought that would mean no more eating out . . . but then I discovered a little secret. There is more than one way to satisfy a wandering palate without losing your shirt in the process. Thanks to my discovery, not only did I get to have my cake and eat it, too, but my social life was greatly enhanced!

My first discovery was hotel lobbies; yes, my sister, there is quite a spread to be had in hotel lobbies in the early evening during cocktail hour. It is *très chic* to sit and look cute noshing on finger foods while sipping your favorite libation. For the cost of a drink or perhaps not—if you are fortunate enough to have an admirer buy a drink for you—you can fill up on hors d'oeuvres and make new friends. Still hungry? Have a salad when you get home. But I doubt that you will be. You'll be amazed at how full you will get from all the outward stimuli of people watching, meeting some new faces, and having a blast with your friends.

Remember, we've already discovered that it is good to be social. Too many of us get in a rut of going to work, church, and home. Then we complain that we're bored. The truth of the matter is that we have become boring people.

Get out, circulate, and find creative options for filling your time as well as your tummy.

So now your limited wallet is pushing you out of the house and stimulating new activities you wouldn't otherwise have considered. Don't stay at home feeling sorry for yourself, noshing on a bunch of stuff that will make you gain weight. Get out, circulate, and find creative options for filling your time as well as your tummy. The more often you have to look cute, the more you will stay on top of your weight so you can get in your outfits too!

Another little secret jewel of a find is lunch specials. Lunch can run anywhere from a half to a third less than dinner at most hotels and fine restaurants. Talk about getting a bigger bang for your buck.

Picture this: I'm sitting at the Ritz having the most lovely salad and soup, just because I can. Why can I? Because I've gone at lunchtime, dahling! You can be so fabulous for little or next to nothing. Most places have wonderful lunchtime specials that are actually better meals. "In what way?" you say. They are actually the right serving amount. For the most part, we all eat way too much food in this country. It doesn't take long to notice that while Europeans eat well, they also consume smaller portions and stay smaller, too, which is the by-product of eating smaller, balanced portions. This is why my other secret is if I eat out in the evening, I go with a friend who is not opposed to sharing. Together we order a full-size salad and entrée and split them both. Two for one, or is it the other way around? If you go to a really nice restaurant, they will even split the courses and put them on separate plates in the kitchen so you don't have to do it yourself in the middle of the restaurant and give other people ideas.

And don't despise those little booklets that come in the mail with coupons for restaurants; there's a lot of fine dining to be had. Or you can log on to restaurant.com for an endless supply of coupons to restaurants, not just in your city but around the world! Each day, they post new specials for particular restaurants. This could become a habit! You can buy fifty-dollar gift cards to these places starting at ten dollars.

Some coupons feature buy-one-dinner-get-one-for-free, so the tab can add up to one you and a friend can split and eat for a fraction of the cost. Make it exciting. Now is the chance to discover new restaurants. One thing I love about

113

Chicago is that generally speaking, the food is great pretty much wherever you go. This is a wonderful opportunity to broaden your knowledge of your local city and what it has to offer, as well as your culinary repertoire. Log on to your local radio stations' Web sites and see what their sponsors have to offer. Sometimes they have coupons for eating out, entertainment, you name it. Then, when going out with a group of friends, why not all meet at one person's house and carpool it together? That way you're only paying for one cab ride or parking spot, and you can split that cost.

Perhaps the best part of lack is that you have to get creative and think outside the box, which will broaden the scope of your world and lead to new adventures.

When you dine out, never underestimate the power of the doggie bag. Echoes of my mother telling me, "There are children starving in Ethiopia!" when I wouldn't eat all my food as a child come back to haunt me whenever I can't finish my entrée. Dutifully, I package up the remains and carry them home. Gratefully, I eat them the next day for lunch or dinner. By then, they are even yummier after having an evening for the seasonings to take root. Leftovers are two meals for the price of one, and that's a delicious meal you can't afford to throw away.

Last but certainly not least, accept invitations. Most social galas and gatherings for causes usually have a wonderful spread. Recently I was invited to the opening of the Trump Tower spa. All of the leading ladies of the city were there. The appetizers were marvelous, and the guest list was even more divine. It was the place to be for making serious connections.

On top of it all, everyone attending got a free thirty-day pass to the spa!

The next weekend there was a fund-raiser at the Merchandise Mart to raise money for another charity. Tickets were twenty-five dollars. Once inside, you could gaze at different dining décor displays, bid on a silent auction, network, and sample food from ten different restaurants! It made for a fun and filling afternoon. Plus all the restaurants gave out coupons you could use to dine with them again. Talk about a tasty deal! How awesome is that? I never knew not having money could be so much fun! Perhaps the best part of lack is that you have to get creative and think outside the box, which will broaden the scope of your world and lead to new adventures. And who wouldn't want to experience that?!

DIVA REVELATION

Remember that sometimes reaching beyond your present boundaries and surroundings can yield chance meetings that can lead to a profitable exchange as well as give you a wealth of rich experiences. As the Scripture says, rise up, daughter, shake the dust off, and strengthen your arms.[1] Sitting at home alone only makes for a very bad pity party. Get out of the house. Start a club with a few friends to find new and fun places to go, eat, and socialize. Be intentional in your pursuit of new experiences. And remember that one good adventure will surely lead to another. Sometimes the best things in life really are for free or at least cost a lot less than you thought. And no matter what, a girl's gotta eat!

WHAT'S A DIVA TO DO?

- Subscribe to a good social network that posts events online. That way you can stay in the know.

- Begin to answer some of the invitations you previously threw away.

- Step out of your comfort zone, and make some new friends.

- Carefully select a few new haunts for noshing after work.

17

COUNTING ON THE
KINDNESS OF STRANGERS

EVEN BEFORE MY finances evaporated, I had established a
very important shopping ritual. At the beginning of every
season, I would go to see what the fashion landscape was for
the year. I'd stop, I'd admire, I'd fondle, but I'd never buy. I'd
wait. . . . You see, I had learned a very valuable secret about
shopping. What goes up must come down. I was (and still
am) willing to take my chances. Nothing would make me
more evil than paying full price for something, only to return
to the store months later to see it reduced to less than half of

what I paid for it. I would definitely not feel warm and fuzzy about that at all.

I learned a long time ago that, in order to get my fashion fix, I needed the inside scoop. I needed a heads-up, if you will, so I could know when things were about to go on sale and reserve my booty. So I made friends with Sarah, Tony, Victoria, and Mrs. Watson . . . the salespeople in the various departments; my friends could let me know when things were about to be put on sale. Sarah would call me and whisper very conspiratorially into the phone, "They're about to put that navy suit you liked on sale, 60 percent off, but you know . . . they're going to do an additional 15 percent off next Wednesday. Do you want me to just put it on hold for you?" See what I mean about the huge markup on this stuff? Just think, if a store is marking an outfit down that low and still making money, how much did the outfit cost them in the first place? Because I started off sewing my own clothes, I can't bear to pay a lot of money for an outfit, because I know how much it really cost to make it. It's the same with imported products. I shop in the markets of Africa. When I price African art here, I practically hyperventilate! The markup is unbelievable. So again, I wait and cart things home on the plane one piece at a time.

But this is where relationships can work for you. Make friends with salespeople. They will look out for you. Shop with the same person all the time. They will learn your taste, and even when you haven't been to the store, they will call when something goes on sale that they think you will like. They all have my phone number. My girl Sarah would call and say, "There is a blouse here that you need in your life, so I put it to the side for you. When can you come down and take a look at it?" Then there's Tony: "Hey, lady, I just spotted a really nice pump that has a heel you can walk in." He knew I couldn't walk on tall heels because of my knee injury from a car accident. And then there's my dear Victoria, who hides things for me when she knows the sale is coming.

Not only do my "friends" hide away impending sale items, but they are also honest with me about what I should and shouldn't wear. Tony would turn up his nose and say, "Nah, that shoe is not worth the money, and don't you have something like that already anyway? I think you should wait." They are not interested in just one short-term sale and commission. They understand that being in relationship with their customers ensures many more sales to come. I have to admit that when times were more plentiful, I might not have really needed the item they had expressed so much glee over securing for me, but I bought it anyway because I didn't want to discourage them. As I said, that was in days of plenty. Now that times are leaner, my friends are understanding and much more selective when it comes to calling me. They have honored my shopping fast and not tempted me because our relationship has grown beyond just shopper to salesperson.

Just think, if a store is marking an outfit down that low and still making money, how much did the outfit cost them in the first place?

When you take the time to be interested in the people serving you—whether you are at a restaurant, boutique, or the mechanic's—a little bit of nice can go a long way and save you tons of money. When you take the time to make others feel significant, they want to go the extra mile for you and extend favor to you that is not offered to others who treat them as mere servants. Ask those who serve you how they are doing. Be genuinely interested. Kindness saves you more than grief and aggravation; it can save you dollars because other people are looking out for you.

I've eaten at restaurants and had most of my meal for free because I started asking the server about herself. Next thing I knew, I had free appetizers, drinks, dessert. . . .

My mechanic has adopted me and watches over my car like he's my father. Now when I go to drop my car off, he invites me in for tea. He works on my car for the cost of the parts. How do I know? I took my car to the dealership once when I was having a problem with it and almost fainted when they gave me the estimate for repair. I then took it to my friend, who charged me one-third of the price! Once there was a light on that I was concerned about. He advised me to wait to see if it would go off instead of spending money for a problem that might correct itself. At the dealership they wanted me to spend money to correct a problem that did indeed correct itself after a good drive on the highway, as my friend had suggested.

When you take the time to be interested in the people serving you—whether you are at a restaurant, boutique, or the mechanic's—a little bit of nice can go a long way and save you tons of money.

Relationship truly makes a difference in your bank account. No one will care about the money you have to spend until they care about you.

DIVA REVELATION

Those who serve you should never be treated as servants. The more dignity you give to those who work in the service industry, the more pride they will take in their work and the more joyfully they will see to your needs. The more difficult you make it for them to help you, the less cooperation you will receive and the higher your tab will be. Kindness is a savings account that costs you nothing. So be nice. It just makes sense—or is that cents?

WHAT'S A DIVA TO DO?

- Select your primary venues for the places where you do business.

- Locate someone who has been a fixture there. Seek them out and ask them if they will be your special contact.

- Be consistent with those who serve you. Never, ever buy when things are not on sale. You will set the standard for what they think you can afford.

- Do not treat those who serve you like servants. Give them significance by being kind, caring, and considerate.

- Don't make it difficult to serve you. Be clear about what you want, and be honest in your transactions.

18

DAMSELS AND KNIGHTS

I HAVE TO tell you something else that I observed as a result of my financial crisis. (It's a bit quirky but really interesting.) During my lean days, I noticed something a little different about my men friends. All of a sudden, these normally laid-back brothers kicked into high-gear rescue mode. They left me scratching my head, wondering what to make of the change.

I got to thinking! Since I'm of the relationship-expert persuasion, I have heard all the complaints about men being intimidated by strong, successful women. I think these complaints are based on the premise that men need to feel needed.

I have long held to the opinion that men do not have a problem with successful women, unless those women spend so much time celebrating themselves that there is no room left for them to be admired by anyone else. And that's fair for a man—or anyone—not to want to be with someone who admires herself and touts her accomplishments constantly. Even I get bored when someone goes on and on about everything they've ever done. It's downright obnoxious. Let your works speak for themselves, and move on. Nothing is more attractive than the person who has accomplished major stuff yet leaves the job of sharing her success to other people. People who are overly impressed with themselves are totally unattractive.

I have long held the opinion that men do not have a problem with successful women, unless those women spend so much time celebrating themselves that there is no room left for them to be admired by anyone else.

I also believe that men don't mind strong women either. You see, there's a thin line between a helpless waif who needs to be rescued financially and physically and a woman who is so masculine in her self-sufficient demeanor that it makes a man question his manhood. Your man wants to know that you can handle life and all it throws at you, because he worries about how you would be able to survive should something ever happen to him. He doesn't want to think that you wouldn't be able to fend for yourself and his children. However—and this is a big however—he doesn't want to feel as if he is dealing with another man. He doesn't want to be in a contest with his woman on basic functions that he would love to do for her.

Can you fix your car? That's a beautiful thing if your man is nowhere to be found. If he can be reached, by all means, let the man handle it. Every man secretly longs to be his woman's hero—to take care of her and be her knight in shining armor. So here is the easy prescription for this: When he's not around, handle your business. When he is around, bat those lashes, girl, and send brother man to work! He'll love every minute of it.

I was stranded at the airport with no money. The money my driver friend had given me a few chapters ago had been spent on paying for my luggage to be checked. Now I needed a ride home but had no money to get there. I started calling all my friends. No one answered. I called a male friend of mine in a last-ditch effort, not really anticipating any help from him. This was the same man I had allowed to drive my car for a week, and he had the nerve to ask me for money to wash it! You know the type, fine as wine and used to women falling all over him and spoiling him. I had written him off, but now I was in a jam, so I called him as a last resort and hoped against hope. Boy, was I surprised! He told me he was already in bed but would take care of it. A few minutes later he called me back. He had hired a limo to take me home! You could have knocked me over with a feather. Before hanging up, he instructed me to call and let him know I had gotten home safely, and he followed up in a text saying, "Think of me as you fall asleep." Well! He was always trying to get his flirt on. . . . I didn't know he had it in him, but then I realized I had never given him the opportunity to show me before.

This was when I realized I was learning more than just

financial wisdom during my crunch—I was learning how important it was to a man to feel like a hero on a whole other level! Several of my other male friends began calling regularly to see if I needed anything. Offering to take me to dinner, coming over to do odd jobs around the house, giving me money . . . of course, I didn't take advantage of the situation, but it was good to know that chivalry was not dead. It was alive and looking awfully good!

It was around this time that one of my friends asked me, "How do you get all these men to do things for you? I can't get my brother to come over and put in a new lightbulb at my place!" I replied, "I guess for me there is no shame in needing help. I simply ask." Asking can be the hardest thing a self-made, self-sufficient diva will ever have to learn to do. But for everything you don't ask for, you'll have to find a way to make it happen yourself, and that can grow wearisome after a while. Once again I will remind you that we were not created to function in a vacuum or navigate through life without any help or assistance. Sometimes the simplest way to get the help you need is to just ask! People love to help. It makes them feel significant, and who doesn't respond positively to that?

Asking can be the hardest thing a self-made, self-sufficient diva will ever have to learn to do. But for everything you don't ask for, you'll have to find a way to make it happen yourself, and that can grow wearisome after a while.

Who knows, perhaps it's in our most needy and vulnerable moments that we are finally open to love. When we are way past being impressed with ourselves, we can finally see what others have to offer.

As we take note, we begin to build up others by making them feel valuable, and they truly do make amazing contributions to our world. Quiet as it is kept, behind the facade of every independent woman is a worn-out woman who wonders why she has to do it all. The answer? You don't. Don't wait until you're broke to find that out.

So let a man be a man and step up to the plate. They say water seeks its own level, and I would dare to say that men have abdicated for the most part on being gallant because we have allowed them to. When we raise the bar, they gladly rise to the occasion. So put your wallet away, and let that man pay for your meal, pull out your chair, drive you home no matter how far away you live, and see you safely to your door. You'll be the richer and happier for it.

DIVA REVELATION

Perhaps many say they don't need a man because they are afraid they won't find one. Could it be that we just aren't allowing the ones before us to be who they really are? Think again and resist the urge to be superwoman and put away that cape—especially if it has holes in it!

WHAT'S A DIVA TO DO?

- When a man's around, do absolutely nothing that detracts from him being the man you've been looking for.

- For those deeply entrenched in "independence," try this little experiment: Call a male friend and ask him to do something for you—take a look at your car, whatever! Don't hint. Ask. Don't demand. Ask nicely. Then trip all over yourself with appreciation when he does it. Know what he'll do? Unless he's lazy, he'll grin a lot and ask you what else you need him to do. I'd bet you a million dollars that this would be his reaction, but I don't have a million dollars!

19

KEEPING UP
APPEARANCES

THEY SAY YOU can't judge a book by its cover, but unfortunately many do. So are appearances important? I would say yes, to a specific degree—that degree being that a woman should look good enough to gain entry to where she needs to go, but nothing about her appearance should distract from the woman she really is.

Sometimes you can look too good. Too pulled together. Too expensive. This is when people resist you. Don't want to help you. Why? Because you don't look as if you need anything! I think those who have old money have learned this.

Have you ever noticed that people who have had money for a long time—as in generations of their families—generally tend to be very low key? They've got nothing left to prove. No need to be conspicuously fashionable, wealthy or otherwise. Look at Warren Buffett. He still has the same house he had before he blew up financially. Still driving a nondescript car . . . giving all his money away to charity. He definitely owns his money. His money does not own him. And hey, after you get to the place where you have more money than you can spend without getting ridiculous, there's nothing left to do but try to save a portion of the world. I'm not mad at him about that. Hats off to him and folks like Bill and Melinda Gates, who put their money where their hearts are.

Someone told me that, if you walk around looking as if you don't need anything, no one will give you anything. This can be a two-edged sword. The balance is to look as if you qualify to walk among those who have wealth and position without advertising it. Those who know don't need to see the label; they just know. However, most of the haves that are over having what they have are fearless fashion rebels in the sense that they just boldly make their own statements. They dictate the trends that everyone else follows. And as Oprah was quick to reveal on her show several years ago, they are not scampering off to purchase insanely expensive frocks from quintessential designers. They borrow these things for affairs or rent them and return them, or better still, receive them as gratis from the designer who knows the benefit of making them his or her walking advertisement. Don't get it twisted, girlfriend. Folks who have sense are not blowing their fortunes on what they have on their backs, and you shouldn't be either—even if you have tons of money.

But now that you don't, let's talk about why you did blow money to keep up appearances. Why is it important to you to look a certain way? There was a time in my life that I would not answer my door or go outside of it unless I was completely coiffed and painted. I allowed no one to see me in a less-than-perfect state. What liberated me lies somewhere between Oprah daring to be on TV with no makeup and the revelation that I had issues with myself that I needed to conquer. When I finally realized that I was not my makeup, hair, and clothing, I was set free to be me and even face my public au naturel from time to time.

Folks who have sense are not blowing their fortunes on what they have on their backs, and you shouldn't be either—even if you have tons of money.

I've had to deal with my appearance issues on many levels. I remember my publisher teasingly asking me if I possessed a pair of jeans to wear on a fishing trip when I came to visit him in Oregon. I snuck and bought a pair before the trip just to prove to him I could be more casual than he imagined. Some of my appearance issues were partly due to my upbringing. My mother had cautioned me enough times that you never knew who you would run into; she had told me this so much that I never left the house unless I was completely put together and looking as if I were ready to attend something far more formal than what I was actually going to. But beyond that, it was easy for me to wrap my self-esteem around a piece of designer somethin' somethin' and feel a whole lot better about myself. That's the part I needed to get over, and you may need to also. Because dressing to impress others or simply to boost your self-esteem may win you some admiration, but it will get you far more bills than favor, I conclude.

So, my sister, let's examine your shopping habits. Figure out where they might have run amok and taken your money with them. It's time to get a new attitude. Are you a moderate shopper, an intentional shopper, or a shopaholic? The moderate shopper can enjoy an afternoon out shopping with the girls and come away with a few purchases that don't threaten to break her bank. The intentional shopper only goes shopping for what she needs and sticks to her list. The shopaholic shops for no reason at all. It is an addiction. The first two shoppers are okay if you're not blowing your budget, but there are more shopaholics on the loose than one cares to admit. Shopaholics are those who actually get an adrenaline rush from purchasing things whether they need them or not.

It is only those who don't know their own names or values that seek validation from the labels of others.

This is what we need to stop. Like a ruptured artery, this habit can drain your finances and literally kill your budget. Now if you're still battling personal demons and the need to still be fabulous—and I pray you're on the road to recovery here, too—there are ways to still look as if you are not living in the red. Some of the things I share with you may surprise you, so you can't be a snob. You have to cast out all notions of what you are now and look at this as an exciting approach to shopping. Kind of like a treasure hunt. And trust me, you are a lot closer to the treasure you are looking for than you know!

Michelle Obama has liberated women all over the world by unabashedly courting designers from Michael Kors to J. Crew without apologizing for being off-the-rack one minute and high couture the next. This is the best example of my point that one doesn't always have to lose her shirt in order to wear the right dress. So if you're ready for a change to come to your closet, read on.

DIVA REVELATION

It is only those who don't know their own names or values that seek validation from the labels of others. Until you find delightful confidence in your own brand of uniqueness, you will break the bank struggling to define yourself with symbols of status that are simply that—hollow representations of someone else's achievements (namely, getting your money!). Like the singer who can't sing and fills the stage with dancers to distract us from his or her lack of talent, clothing can be more of a distraction and disguise to hide a lack of substance. It costs far less to work on the content of our character than on draping our frame with expensive fare. At the end of the day, being comfortable in the skin and the clothing you are in, label or no label, is priceless.

WHAT'S A DIVA TO DO?

- Take a good, hard look at the contents of your closet.

- Be honest about why you bought each item. Try to separate your items into two piles: basic necessity items and dress-to-impress pieces. (You can have a third pile reserved for "I just liked it," but try to put items in the basic or dress-to-impress piles.)

- Be honest with yourself. Look at each piece in your dress-to-impress pile and ask yourself, *Was the outcome of my appearance in that garment worth the price I paid?* Where could your money have been better spent? How else could you have impressed your audience? Mm-hmm, I thought so.

20

HOW TO GO SHOPPING IN YOUR CLOSET

MY GIRLFRIEND DAWN went on a shopping fast for a year awhile back. At the end of the year, she used the money she had saved to buy a piece of property! Yeah, girl, all that shopping adds up. If you're a woman, there is a bit of a hoarder in you somewhere, unless you are the other extreme—that being a neat freak. For the most part because of our nesting instincts, most women have a tendency to always have a little extra something lying around. It all depends on what your pleasure is. It can range from shoes to bath products; there is something you have backstock in. So my first challenge to you is not to go shopping for any nonessentials for six months. You guessed it—the month of saying no from chapter 9 was a setup for this next exercise. If you can wrap your head around the concept of a year, go for it, but I want to keep the bar low in order to keep more people on board. Now the next step for you is to take inventory of what you already have. You will be amazed at what you find.

Let's go down the list together. You probably have tons of stuff you love. Things you forgot you had. Products you never touched because you kept buying more. Let me tell you that when I disciplined myself not to buy another bottle of bath gel, body lotion and potions, shampoo, or conditioner until I had used every bottle I already had, it took me over a year to run out! And that was after I had sent a box of unopened toiletries to an orphanage in Haiti. Mm-hmm, it is truly shameful. But I'm a sucker for anything that smells and feels good. I am a total hedonist in that regard. And yet, I am a creature of habit. I gravitate back to my two favorite scents and basically live there—shunning all the new discoveries I've dragged home because I was caught up in a whim of fanciful scents at the time. And when I got home and realized I didn't need the new scent, I was kind of stuck with it; I mean, who is going to take the time to return a bottle of bath gel to the store? That's what all the infomercial people bargain on when they suck you into buying all that stuff on television. It's so gracious of them to offer to give you your money back if you don't like the product or didn't get the results you were hoping for, isn't it? Don't be fooled: They know that by the time you get around to realizing you are not using the product or you don't like it, the box is long gone and so is your will to return it. Therefore, we all have some piece of workout equipment or makeup or something we bought in the middle of the night that has taken on a life of its own now that we've see the light of day. And let's not even start talking about when the repeat shippings kick in because we forgot to cancel the membership after we tried the first round of product! I hope you're getting the picture.

The shopping fast is meant to clean your palate and give you a new perspective on your purchases. As my friend Holly says, you will soon be able to discern whether it is a "need or a greed." So now we will be able to more aptly apply ourselves to the principle of "waste not, want not."

The shopping fast is meant to clean your palate and give you a new perspective on your purchases.

A long-standing tradition I've had over the years is to purge my closet yearly. I try to stick to the rule that if I haven't worn a piece of clothing in a year, out it goes. To be honest, it doesn't always work, but sometimes it does. My friends love this rule. Yearly they gather as if awaiting some epic event. I usually stack my things into piles I've allocated for each of them according to what I know they like; they can exchange among themselves if they like something in another friend's pile. However, in financially strapped times, I was forced to do things differently. I discovered there was hidden wealth in my closet!

After sorting through all the things I was willing to get rid of, I pulled a few choice pieces for my friends, took the rest to the cleaners, and sent them off to the consignment shops.

Mm-hmm, depending on the piece, you can make a nice piece of change from your castoffs. Different consignment shops have different rules for what they will accept and the percentages they pay once they've sold your garments, but let me tell you, the shekels add up quickly. Not only is it great to get back some of the money you spent on your garments, but it can be downright fun! A word of caution: Stick to taking your clothes and dropping them off, and do not look to the left or right on your way back out. Remember that you came to sell, not to buy. Another way you can do it if you live in an apartment complex is to have a sidewalk sale in the hallway. Put up a sign and make it a neighborly party. Whoohoo! Last but certainly not least is eBay. Post it and get rid of it.

These money-making tips can only work if you've bought well over the years. I have a simple shopping rule: Invest in classics; purchase inexpensive to cheap fads. I don't spend a lot of money on the things that are only going to last a season. For the classics, I will pay a bit more while sticking to my blanket rule that it must be on sale. I once purchased a designer suit for less than a tenth of the price at the end of the season. At the beginning of the season the jacket alone had been two thousand dollars! Do you know how sick I would have felt if I had purchased it at that price and then returned to see it marked down to nearly nothing? I thought you knew! To this end, most of my things are well over ten years old, and I'm still wearing them because they are quality pieces, made from good fabric, that never go out of style (hence the word *classic*). Let's face it: You can buy the same inexpensive article five times because it doesn't last as long, or you can take the total of those five purchases and buy one good thing that will outlast the five you had to keep replacing. Usually my hips spread beyond the *wearability* of my clothes first before the fabric does. All that to say that if you buy well, when you're ready to part with it, you can actually get some of your money back.

If you're like me, you probably have at least three different sizes of clothes in your wardrobe—the size you are in currently; the size your weight has dropped to before; and the sizes you hope and pray you will be able to get back into some fine day. Take a deep breath and get rid of everything you cannot wear. Your great reward, should you ever lose that much weight again, will be new clothes, and you would have earned them. In the meantime, they are merely taking up space, and you could be making money, girl!

Be a work of art, and no matter what you wear, you will look oh so fabulous.

DIVA REVELATION

Your future will never squeeze into your past, so give yourself a present and get rid of the old to make room for the new— or to just have a bit more room, period! Part of making room for wealth is to literally make room. There is something about our unwillingness to let go that cuts off the flow of all that wants to come our way. Remember, you are not what you wear. Your outer trappings should never distract from your internal beauty. Therefore, don't go in the hole to paint a picture that doesn't need to be rendered anyway. Be a work of art, and no matter what you wear, you will look oh so fabulous.

WHAT'S A DIVA TO DO?

- Declare a shopping fast—you pick the length of it, but it should hurt slightly, or it's not a fast. This can be applied to any area where you have a tendency to overindulge. From clothing, to products, to food— whatever you hoard you need to finish before you buy again.

- Clean out your closet. Sort a pile for friends and/or charity. (Please don't give away things you would not want to be given.) Sort a pile for sale.

- Google consignment shops in your area to find out their requirements.

21

THE SECRET TO SELF-GRATIFICATION

FOR THOSE WHO are still having a panic attack from the last chapter on fasting from shopping for six months to a year, I am going to give you a little relief. It is a well-known fact that if you can get past the third day of not eating food, you will be able to successfully stay on track with fasting. The first phase is always the most difficult. The flesh is screaming for everything you ever thought you might like to eat, whether you want it or not; hunger makes everything look good. Your eyes become bigger than your stomach, and you reach for empty calories that do you no good. The same is true with shopping. All of a sudden the top or pair of shoes you had been searching for forever will appear magically and be on sale to boot! Everything inside you will scream that you need just one more thing before you start your shopping fast. The fear that your treasured find won't be there once your fast has ended will cause you to waver.

You have to stay strong. You have to find creative ways to stick to your guns. Extreme denial is never a good thing. It only leads to bingeing at some point. What we are trying to get to here is a beautiful thing called balance. I was trying to understand one day the concept behind the Scripture that says, "Let no man say when he is tempted, I am tempted of God: for God cannot be tempted."[1] Now I know He is God and everything, but I was curious as to why He couldn't be tempted. Then the understanding dawned on me: Because He created everything and owns everything, He doesn't need anything else! Everything He wants He already has, except for those who aren't interested in having a relationship with Him. Therefore nothing tempts Him.

If we also adopt the mentality that we have everything we need already (and the truth of the matter is we do), we will be able to take or leave any "temptations" we encounter. If I was completely happy with the collection of black shoes I had, I wouldn't be interested in buying another pair, even if they were on sale. Why? Because I had already completed my black shoe collection! You might say to me, "But, Michelle, my black shoes don't have a bow on them like the pair I just saw!" Big deal. Go buy some bows and slap them on the ones you already have. Or get real with yourself and ask, *Did I*

even think about some bows on my shoes until I saw that pair?
Alrighty then! Face it, girl—you don't need them.

There are other ways to get around the need to have
something new. It's called working with what you already
have. For instance, grab that pair of slacks you haven't worn
because your hips have spread. Take those pants to the cleaners or your local tailor and have them open
up the legs and make you a nice tapered
skirt! Voilà! You now officially have something new for a fraction of the cost of an off-
the-rack purchase.

If we can adopt the mentality that we have everything we need already (and the truth of the matter is we do), we will be able to take or leave any "temptations" we encounter.

And now that you have cleaned out your
closet (you did follow my directions from
the previous chapter, right?) and you can see
what is in it, look again at what you have.
What could use an extreme makeover and be
good for another spin on the catwalk? Perhaps you could shorten the sleeves on that
jacket to three-quarter length or to the elbow for a new spin.
Maybe you can take the sleeves off altogether, belt it, and get
a smart vested look out of it. Perhaps that A-line dress can be
slimmed down into a tapered look that takes pounds off your
hips when you wear it. The cuffs could come out of those
slacks. You could add some fabulous pins to a blouse or jacket
to spruce it up. Add a touch of lace or an appliqué to something to jazz it up. Sometimes it's as simple as taking the time
to coordinate new combinations with what you already have.
My girlfriend Pamela came over and went through my closet
and mixed and matched some things I would never have put

together. When I stepped out in one of her new combinations, I got so many compliments, I was walking on cloud nine by the time I made it home. Again, giving your clothes a makeover is another fun thing you can do with friends. (We're back to that community again!) Even when it comes to our wardrobes, two heads have always been better than one. So many options, what's a girl to do? Look fabulous, what else?

The same thing applies to your jewelry—there's so much opportunity in your little jewelry box. Gather up all your little-girl jewelry that's sitting in your jewelry case and sell it. Or trade it in for a better piece. Or melt it down and make yourself another piece inexpensively. I had two bracelets I never wore melted down and had a ring made for $100 that looked like a designer ring. Can you say $100 sounds a whole lot better than $2,100, the actual price of the ring I duplicated? Mm-hmm, I thought you knew! In Chicago, the International Gem & Jewelry Show and the TransWorld jewelry show come to town quarterly. This is where the world of wholesale jewelry, clothing, and accessories goes to a whole new level. I gathered up a small pouch of rings and things I hadn't worn in forever, and off to the show I went. After visiting several booths with my wares, I emerged victorious with enough cash to pay one month's mortgage and a new pair of earrings I would never have been able to afford as a bonus! I'm still smiling.

I've come to learn that my longing for things is closely tied to my spiritual longing for a greater connection with God, which is completion on a higher level.

If you are still having withdrawal symptoms and really need to shop, why not have a swap party? This is where you call up all your friends who have as marvelous a clothing selection as yourself—in your size, of course. You all gather with purges from your respective closets in hand, and then you exchange. Here's your chance to get that blouse your girlfriend had on that you secretly coveted—and you don't have to spend a dime! Add some refreshments to the mix, and it's an all-out party where you leave with more than good feelings.

I've discovered that one woman's trash is another woman's treasure. What I've gotten sick of is a new treasure to someone else who didn't have it and vice versa. The thing I've discovered is that the dress I thought I couldn't part with is quickly forgotten once I've let it go. I can't tell you how many times I've complimented one of my friends on an outfit they were wearing for them to laughingly tell me, "I guess you would like it. I got it from you!" I had completely forgotten. Or maybe they just looked better in it than I did . . . hmmm. . . . At any rate, it is a good feeling to bless others, and it's even better to get something new for free!

DIVA REVELATION

Could it be that the constant quest for something new speaks to something deeper? I've come to learn that my longing for things is closely tied to my spiritual longing for a greater connection with God, which is completion on a higher level. The more layers I add to my external, the more the vacuum within seems to grow. I find that when I finally buckle down and fast from food, my longing for "junk" and things that are not healthy wanes rapidly; likewise, I've found that as I discipline myself not to shop, I discover more of what I already have, and I find joy in unexpected places. And that is true fulfillment. Got it? You'll be so full you will be filled, as in lacking nothing.

WHAT'S A DIVA TO DO?

- Take another inventory of your closet, now that it is condensed. (And if you didn't downsize that closet from last chapter, get to it!) You might even want to write down the things you find in your closet and categorize them.

- Organize your closet so you can find things easier. Part of the reason we feel we need more clothes is because we don't know what we already have.

- Pull the things that need an extreme makeover.

- Try some new combinations. Take photos and make a mini-catalog for yourself.

- Have a swap party.

- Don't focus on what you don't have. Focus on what you do have.

22

COUPONS, POINTS, AND SALES, OH MY!

HOPEFULLY YOUR SHOPPING fast has cleansed your shopping palate and made you look at shopping from a whole new perspective. Yes, ladies, it's time to look at how to get the biggest bang for your buck if you must indulge in retail therapy. It's called bargain shopping. Just the thought of a good bargain can get my pulse racing, I tell ya! Bargains can be a lifesaver when you have designer tastes and a resale-shop budget. There are so many ways to rack up major savings with coupons and to accumulate points to acquire things for free—it's ridiculous.

First of all, you need to know the seasons for sales. If you are buying classic pieces, you can afford to wait until the end of the season to acquire a piece that you will wear for years to come. I usually scope out everything I like at the beginning of the season, pray over it, and tell it to stay until sale time. My salesclerks always laugh at me when I do this, but more often than not, my desired item is still there at the end of the season. I have been known to collect an entire suit piece by piece in my travels. "How do you do that?" Sarah, my saleslady at the old Marshall Field's, would always say. I recall getting all four pieces of a Michael Kors suit at three different stores in two different cities. By the time I was done, I had gotten all four pieces for the original cost of the slacks! "Amazing," Sarah muttered as I happily scooped up a skirt that went with the whole ensemble after someone else returned it; I got it at 90 percent off. It was a major coup. If I could live in Michael Kors and Donna Karan, I would, but the only way it's possible for this girl is through serious sales and points.

Speaking of points, you've got to love the American Express Classic Card on several levels. First, it keeps you honest. When you get the bill, you have to pay it, so you can't resort to magical thinking with this card. You can only spend what you can afford to pay within a month, which is a good thing. In addition, American Express has amazing rewards for their points! Whenever you purchase a certain amount, you receive reward points; you can use these points to get free stuff. I use this card for business, and believe you me, I hoard my points for a long time before using them. I have vacationed on my points; that's right, I've gotten airline tickets, hotel rooms, car rentals, and even a Michael Kors shearling coat with my Amex points. I cashed my points in for gift certificates to Saks Fifth Avenue and walked out with my dream coat for free. Most stores, from expensive to inexpensive, now have some sort of points or card program to garner our loyalty—so investigate what is at your disposal and take advantage!

One Christmas I used points to do all my shopping for gifts. Normally I don't do Christmas gifts. I opt for doing generous birthdays when I have the luxury of focusing on one person versus having to spread the wealth over a large number of people at Christmas. Works for them. Works for me. However, due to points, I felt generous one year. I was able to be Santa without clearing out the bank.

The other beautiful thing is the magical world of cyberspace, where anything can be had for a pittance if you're willing to search. Sites such as overstock.com have slashed prices from 10 to 50 percent on everything from clothing to home furnishings; sometimes the shipping is free, and when it's not, it's usually a minimal fee. On overstock.com, you can bid on things that people return for an even lower price. I also love shopittome.com. You can specify your favorite brands, your size, all your specifics, and they will send you weekly news about sales on your preferences.

Bargains can be a lifesaver when you have designer tastes and a resale-shop budget.

Priceplease.com is another site that will inform you when the price of what you're looking for drops. Gilt.com offers discounts on designer clothing. Bluefly.com also offers discounts on clothes and accessories by designers including Vera Wang and Marc Jacobs. Replicaestore.com is great for finding

knockoffs on the most popular designer bags. Bagborroworsteal
.com and frombagstoriches.com allow you to rent your favorite designer bags for a week or a month. Seventy percent of
your rental fee goes into an equity bank that you can use to
purchase a bag from the outlet section of the site if you so
choose. The site offers up to 70 percent off on new to gently-
loved bags. Zappos.com is shoe heaven on a screen. 6pm.com
offers up to 75 percent off the retail price for shoes, clothing,
and bags. Endless.com offers reduced prices on shoes, bags,
and accessories with free overnight shipping. Shoesale.com
is another one offering an array of shoe savings.

Want to compare prices before you commit? Check out
nextag.com, bizrate.com, and pricegrabber.com. It's always
good to see the full range of choices before making a decision.

There is a virtual world of savings out there if you're willing to take the time to look.

I hate thinking I got a good bargain and then
finding it somewhere else cheaper, don't you?
Another thing you can do is first check out
what you're looking for at the store. Try it on.
Make a note of the exact style name and number so you can be specific in your search. Don't
want to wait for your bargain find online? Print
off the item and the reduced price, return to the store, and ask
them to match the price for you. Most of the time they will!

If you're looking for good fares for traveling, log on to
kayak.com. I love this one because it compares all the fares
from Orbitz and the rest of the travel sites to give you the best
fare. If you travel for work, make sure you sign up for all of
the airline and hotel points programs; most employers will
let you use them for your own personal use. If you can, try

to remain faithful to a specific airline and hotel. Those miles and nights add up to points that can be redeemed for more than trips and hotel stays. Some of them are transferable for gift cards to restaurants and department stores.

Google should be your new BFF. You can search for coupons and free shipping codes on Google for anything that you are purchasing. Of course, eBay can be the ultimate to finding whatever you can dream of. For those who enjoy bidding on things, it can be fun and addictive. However, if you want to sidestep the competition, you can do a search for things you can purchase outright. I've found things on eBay I couldn't find anywhere else. From makeup to clothing, electronics, furniture—whatever, it's there to be found. Retailmenot.com posts coupons daily for all your retail dreams!

There is a virtual world of savings out there if you're willing to take the time to look. The bottom line of this exercise is never to pay the base ticket price for anything. Why not? Because you don't have to. Every penny saved eventually adds up to a dollar, and a dollar to hundreds saved by the time you do the math.

Don't despise shopping clubs and discount cards from your grocery stores and various discount specialty shops like Sephora, Ulta, and DSW. They are faithful to send you coupons for things off or free gifts—again, every penny saved helps! Take the time to find out all the things that are available to you for your specific cards. I do a jig every time I get groceries. I hand over my store card and get savings in return subtracted from my final tally at the checkout.

Lots of your credit cards will give you rewards or points

for purchases that can be used toward services and purchases. Take advantage of those points, because they add up quickly if you stay loyal to a specific store or card. For example, Neiman Marcus gives you points for your purchases. Once you charge over a certain amount in one year, they issue you points that can be turned in for cash to purchase whatever you want. I call this the secret life of the wealthy. Generally speaking, those who have true wealth are also extremely frugal. They know the value of money as well as the things they want to purchase. I believe that one of the reasons the rich get richer and the poor stay poor is because the rich find all of the ways not to spend more money while the poor perish for lack of knowledge. So now that I've pulled your coattail about a few savings options for when you must shop, wise up and buy right. Your bank account depends on it!

DIVA REFLECTION

Along with the ability to make money comes another awesome responsibility. It's called being a wise steward of what you've been given. I once heard someone say that if you don't respect money, it will run from you. This is true. As you watch every dollar you spend, you will gain clarity about the value of the things you are purchasing and gain a new perspective on how to go about getting what you want. There is something about knowing that you shopped responsibly that gives you peace of mind. When you spend unthinkingly for the first asking price, you rob yourself in the long run. Remember that anything you purchase is temporary; therefore, it should never leave a permanent dent in your finances.

WHAT'S A DIVA TO DO?

- Take a responsible approach to shopping.

- Take the time to do your homework, and research your purchases. If it's electronics, read reviews and compare prices before purchasing.

- Use all of your options—coupons, points, and discount codes—to get the best price possible.

- Don't get distracted. Stay on point with what you came to purchase in the first place. Don't get sucked into all the other bargains and blow what you would have saved!

- Tech savvy can equal penny smart when mastered. Make the Google search engine your very best friend.

23

THERE IS NO SHAME IN GENERICS AND OTHER TRADE SECRETS

THERE WAS A TIME you couldn't have paid me to use a generic anything—that is, until I fell on hard times and discovered that sometimes you don't necessarily get what you pay for. In fact, sometimes you can get a whole lot more for a whole lot less. I learned the value of generics from having three dogs. It makes me understand how children who are later or last in birth order sometimes feel like they get cheated. When I got my first dog, Milan, she went to doggie school, she had the best doctor, and she got the collar with all the bling; my second dog, Matisse, got the same luxurious treatment; but by the time I adopted my third bundle of furry love, Micah, he got the hand-me-down leash, he got "homeschooled" by yours truly, and he went to the "county" to be fixed. My heart was big enough to love him, but I didn't have the same type of budget. Then all of my dogs developed allergies. The vet suggested I give them a low-milligram dose of a popular antihistamine. When I went to the drugstore, I made a surprising discovery. I could get either ten tablets of the popular brand or ninety tablets of a generic brand for close to the same price! I picked up both and read the ingredients. I spoke to the pharmacist. Voilà! They had the same ingredients—just different packaging and different names. Talk about things that make you go hmmm . . .

You know my curiosity was now piqued; what else had I been squandering money on needlessly? Of course, in some instances it is still wise to stick with a name you can trust, but in other instances, a name has little to do with what you're getting except to identify who had the impetus to focus on marketing that particular thing. This train of thought goes beyond drugs to items in every category. Food, electronics, cleaning supplies, oh my. . . . There is tons of money to be saved by simply being more discerning about which things need to have a specific label versus what contents or features are needed. Kinda sounds like how I used to choose men. (Can I get an amen or an oh man?) Oh, come on, you know you've been duped by more than one pretty house with no one home. We do judge books, people, and products by their covers (or their brand names), and we can be misled countless times if we don't take the time to check out the contents.

I've become an avid reader of labels. What you don't know can and will hurt you or, in this case, rob you of some extra cash. I recall watching a news special that revealed how some contact lens companies merely change the usage labels on the contacts and raise the price accordingly. At the end of the day, the daily-wear lenses were not different from the extended-wear lenses; you just paid more. Kind of like how placebos work with people. They get better because they think they are taking the medication. The power of the mind is amazing! Advertisers play tricks on our minds every day to make us think we need a specific brand or something won't work as well, taste as good, last as long . . . whatever we think it should do. We are led to believe that if it doesn't have a popular name, it is substandard. However, when in doubt, check with your pharmacist, since some formulations may be different and could affect how effective they are for you.

I've become an avid reader of labels. What you don't know can and will hurt you or, in this case, rob you of some extra cash.

Again, do your research. Google customer reviews on everything from cereal to cleaning solutions to the best HDTV, and see what's up before you give your money away—'cause that's what you're doing if you're spending more than you have to on anything.

The other thing I discovered is that a lot of companies make what they term a "low-end brand." Sort of on the order of what clothing designers do. You know, there's Donna Karan Couture, and then there's DKNY at a more affordable price point. You still get great design and good quality, but they just use more high-end fabric for the couture line along with more detailing and specialized styles. The same holds true for electronics. Sony, for instance, makes electronics under several different names and prices them out at lower price points. You are still getting a quality product with the same good technology. The casing might not be as fancy and distinctive, but it will do what it is supposed to do just as well as the expensive model. However, you need to keep in mind that this has to be researched on a product-by-product basis. Again, do your homework. Sometimes a bargain can turn into a greater expense if you purchase a lemon—so exercise balance in this principle, too.

When it comes to food, everyone's palate is different, but again here, a stewed tomato is a stewed tomato, especially if it is an ingredient in a recipe. Whether it's Hunt's, Del Monte, or the store brand, by the time you add your seasonings for the sauce you're making, you will not taste the difference. However, you might be fussier about things that you can't doctor up, such as ketchup. You cannot move me off my square on this one. When it comes to ketchup, it's got to be Heinz for me.

When it comes to clothing, the definite way to make sure you buy quality every time is to make certain you are dealing with a pure fabric—real cotton, pure linen, or wool without the blend. Lots of blends ball up and give your garment a short life before they look worse for wear. I think you're getting the picture on this exercise.

In Chicago, there's a wholesale district for clothing, hair accessories, handbags, etc. You just have to search it out. You know that fabulous hair barrette you saw downtown for twenty dollars? That same piece will be two to seven dollars at the wholesalers. If you ever get to Dallas, check out Sam Moon. It is the place for all girlie accessories. You can go online if you can't get there to purchase a limited range of things for little to nothing. Keep in mind that, if you're known for wearing designer stuff and serious, real jewelry, when you mix in things that are not, they will be high end by association. It's all in the way you coordinate and place your things.

Last but not least, some of the things you think you need, especially for cleaning, are already in your kitchen cupboard. There's a place beyond generic called using what you have on hand. Log on to eartheasy.com/live_nontoxic_solutions.htm for homemade cleaning solutions. Who'd a thunk you could use vinegar so many different ways?! Did you know newspaper and vinegar will clean glass just as well as Windex and paper towels? Hey, I'm just trying to help a sistah out! Stop spending money and use what you have. One of my favorite stories in the Bible is about when Moses was going back to Egypt to lead the Israelites out

Sometimes we can get stuck on principle and overlook the options that can bless us more and cost us less.

of there. He felt he was ill-equipped for the mission. God says to him, "What do you have in your hand?" Moses says, "Just a stick." God tells him to throw it down, and it turns into a serpent that scares Pharaoh's magicians.[1] Sometimes we're sitting on something more powerful than we know. What's in your hand? The very thing you think doesn't add up to much of anything can hold major surprises and perform some little miracles, too!

DIVA REVELATION

Sometimes we can get stuck on principle and overlook the options that can bless us more and cost us less. The contents will always be far more important than the external package. Sometimes we have to press past the surface of what is before us—whether we're talking people or products, the reward is the same. We come out richer for the knowledge. More than anything, thinking outside the box in more ways than one can introduce us to greater opportunities to experience something new and better than what we've already experienced at less expense on many levels. By being willing to reconsider what is already in our grasp, as well as working with what we already have, we can become more profitable than we ever imagined.

WHAT'S A DIVA TO DO?

- Take a second look at your name-brand items, and see which ones can be replaced by more reasonable substitutes.

- Do your research. Check out ingredients and manu-facturers before making a switch.

- Be resourceful with the things you already have.

- Remember, this is all about cutting expenses. Don't spend money on things you don't have to.

24

PUTTING YOUR BEST FACE FORWARD

LET'S FACE IT, no pun intended, but your face, or *visage*, as the French would say, is what people see first. It is your first impression. Experts say that during economically challenging times, one of the things that never goes down in sales is makeup. Vanity will prevail no matter what! In better days I would march into the department store and boldly purchase top-of-the-line cosmetics and skin care. Trust me—that has changed. And while my face still looks the same, I've changed up my regimen big time.

Again, you do not have to spend as much money as you

would think in order to look beautiful. There are some tried-and-true beauty secrets and products that have been around for a long time, and there is a reason for it. "Such as?" you ask. Well, for one, I don't think anyone would argue that Maybelline still makes some of the best mascara on the planet. They might have spruced up the packaging a bit, but for my money, Great Lash is still a top-of-the-line mascara for a lot less than some of the other high-end mascaras. And that is just the beginning of the goodies you can find at any Walgreens, Walmart, Target, CVS, Rite Aid—whatever is in your neck of the woods.

Back during the days of plenty, I was a die-hard MAC fan, and you still can't tear me away from MAC lipstick or Bobbi Brown concealer and gel eyeliner. I rationalize that the expense is worth it because I know that these products last and save me in the long run, but I've discovered the worth of some other products to replace my expensive taste in toiletries. For cleansing and moisturizing, again you can go back to your kitchen cupboard for surprisingly inexpensive and yummy solutions. Everything from honey to avocados to eggs are all great for the skin. Naturally—without all the extraneous chemicals—you can give yourself an inexpensive facial in the comfort of your home. Log on to natural-cure-guide .com for a free e-book in natural beauty. Other Web sites committed to giving you natural recipes for your hair, skin, and body are naturalbeautyworkshop.com, allnaturalbeauty .us, and natural-healthy-beauty-recipes-and-secrets.com.

To cut cost, but not beauty, I've since traded in my Lancôme eye makeup remover for Johnson's Baby Oil. And don't rule out good old Vaseline. Yes! Remember Vaseline? When I was in school, I used to use it for everything. Removing makeup, for lip gloss, for lotion on my elbows and knees. It's a great emollient and moisturizer when used correctly. I would apply it to my wet skin after a shower, pat dry, and let it sink into my skin. It left such a nice glow and kept my skin feeling moist. But as I got older, I went off in pursuit of other, more expensive lotions and potions. Why? I have no real reason, so I will say simply because I could. Well, I've returned to some basics. And now they have Johnson's Baby Oil Gel. I love it! (And again, it's a mere pittance in comparison to what I was paying for creams.)

There are some great makeup choices that can save you money as well. L'Oréal really is worth it, and so are a few other choice makeups. There's Almay, Cover Girl, Revlon, Neutrogena—depending on your complexion, you're sure to find a great match. If you just have to stick with your more expensive, higher-end products, then search eBay or beauty.com for discounts that can help you keep an expensive habit under control. I found my favorite cleanser on eBay for way less than I was paying for it in the department store. I then found samples, which I purchased for pennies, to keep in my suitcase for when I traveled. I saved a ton not having to buy duplicate products at the regular size. You can also purchase samples of all of your toiletries for your travel case—especially if you are carrying your luggage on the plane. All it takes is one time to cry over a bottle of your favorite perfume or lotion—that is over the approved size— being taken away by security to make you learn an expensive

lesson. While we're on the value of samples, how about purchasing sample sizes of nail lacquer? How many times have
you bought the regular-size bottle, then used it once or left
it around until it grew hard and ugly on you? You better stop
wasting money, girl!

Can I tell you I've discovered that, instead of paying so
much for lip pencils, the ones that go for a dollar at the drugstore or beauty supply shop are just as fabu-
lous and sometimes last longer? Fancy that!
Once you get past names and labels and just
start experimenting with the actual products, you can discover ways around the high
prices. The things you choose to spend more
on should have quality and lasting power.

Once you get past names and labels and just start experimenting with the actual products, you can discover ways around the high prices.

I've also discovered that one of the ways
you can get the most out of your lipsticks is
to use a pill container. You know—the hard
plastic ones with sections for your pills by the day. Scoop
out lipsticks into the sections in the pill container, put the
container in the microwave for ten seconds—long enough to
soften the lipstick down into the pots—and voilà! You have
a lip palette where you can see all of your colors at a glance
and actually use them. Mm-hmm, you know you don't know
half the colors you have, and you probably keep buying the
same color over and over again. It's true you won't use what
you can't see.

Have you broken a blush or an eye shadow before and
just thrown it away? That's money gone. Instead of throwing away broken cosmetics, just pour a little bit of alcohol

on the crumbles. Mash them back down into a solid shape and let them air dry. Again, we can't afford to throw anything away. You can stretch out the life of your foundation by mixing it with your moisturizer before applying. That way you are using less, and it can last longer. As for body lotions, I've found my favorite scents in oil or mixed a few spritzes of my favorite fragrance with Johnson's Baby Oil Gel. It makes the scent subtle, but it sticks with me all day. I'm sure that as you start experimenting on your own, you'll come up with even more options for looking, feeling, and smelling beautiful.

When something is expensive in France, they say it is *très cher*, or "very dear." You shouldn't have to break the bank to look beautiful. If that is the case, this means way too much emphasis is being put on externals in order to distract from the beauty we are lacking within. In the realm of makeup, less is always more. However, anger, bitterness, jealousy, unforgiveness, stress, and depression are all things that can change your countenance and overshadow even the best makeup application. So let your regimen begin from within. Your true self should dominate your facade and be the real beautifier. Remember, makeup was never meant to be costly or to be a mask; it should enhance your natural beauty. And nothing is more beautiful than a woman who knows she can pay her bills. To me, that is truly *très cher*—very dear.

> You shouldn't have to break the bank to look beautiful.

DIVA REVELATION

Let's face it. A girl has to put her best face forward in order to make it in life. But if your insides don't live up to the outside, it's all in vain. I find that the uglier you feel, the more makeup gets applied. It took me years to face the world with a clean face, but my boldness was in direct proportion to my inner peace. Lipstick cannot hide sarcasm and negativity. Eye shadow will only highlight hardness and detachment. Are you getting the vision? As you release the things that mar your appearance and remove stress from your life, you will have a beautiful palette to enhance, not paint over. And that is beauty at its finest.

WHAT'S A DIVA TO DO?

- Take a moment to make a list of the things you need to complete your toilette. Everyone's beauty regimen is different. What do you need? Cleanser, moisturizer . . . ?

- Take inventory of what you have already.

- Check out the Web sites I've shared to find bargain prices and discounts.

- Have a party with friends to experiment with some of the natural options. You can mix masks and lotions and try them out together. Kind of like a Mary Kay party!

- Take the time to think beautiful thoughts. Let them saturate your heart and put a natural light in your eyes.

- Need a wash, cut, color, and blow dry? Look up your local beauty school for beauty services that range from nothing to pennies! The same holds true for manicures, dental work, and massages. The students are under the supervision of their instructors, so the quality of the work is usually very good. If there is a hair product manufacturer in your city, that is even better! They usually have a test beauty salon that offers services for free.

25

STICKING CLOSE
TO HOME

ONE THING YOU learn during times of economic stress is that home is not only where the heart is, but it's where true wealth and tremendous savings are to be found. There was a time when I was ruled by wanderlust. I could leave the house at nine in the morning and not get home until after nine at night. Why? Simply because I could. I had no obligations, nothing that required me to be home by a specific time. Such is the life of a liberated single woman. My life and my time were mine to spend as I pleased, or so I thought. Little did I realize that my capricious nature was more than fun—it was expensive.

Oh, it was never my intention to stay out that long. But life happens, if you know what I mean. It would start off innocently enough, meeting a friend for breakfast. This would then transition into a stroll down a street that happened to have some new boutique I had not discovered yet. After a squeal of delight, in I would swoop to sample all their wares up-close and personal. After spending so much time touching and oohing and aahing, well, I had to buy *something* after taking up the lonely salesclerk's time. If I discovered I didn't need it later, I could always delegate it to the gift pile.

On my way out of the shop, I would glance at my watch. *My, where did the time go?* All of this shopping had only made me hungry all over again. So it was off in search of lunch after locating someone to join me. After lunch, it was off to more mindless meandering. Walking through a book store, I picked up a couple of magazines and a CD. A shoe sale! I needed another pair of black flats. (Not really, but could a girl ever have too many black shoes?)

Chaos and too much spontaneity breed expensive distractions that one really doesn't need.

Well, time and money do fly when you're having fun. Now several shopping bags later, it was off to the movies with a friend followed by dinner, topped off with dessert! As I fell in a satisfied heap on my couch later that night, I was stuffed, but my finances were a lot slimmer.

Then life changed for me. I got a dog. Then I got another dog. And another. That is another long story that took an entire book to relay, so get a copy of *Lessons from a Girl's Best Friend* by yours truly. When lady Milan, my shih tzu, moved in, she established rules. She would tolerate my absence from home in four-hour intervals. After that . . . well, the house may be up for grabs. When Matisse came along, he seconded the motion, and Micah, the youngest, definitely yelped his agreement. Suddenly, I found myself curtailing my activities. I had to get home. I had little bundles of love waiting for me! They expected dinner and a nice walk. They required time and attention. It was all rather grounding and revealing. The more time I spent at home, the less money I spent. A sense of order began to settle into my life. This was when I realized that chaos and too much spontaneity breed expensive distractions that one really doesn't need.

I believe that a lot of people don't like to go home because they either haven't taken the time to make it a home or they don't want to face the fact that there is nothing to go home to. For me, this was true. After traveling and being surrounded by love and appreciation for the work I do, my house was loudly silent upon my return. I ran from the silence, but it cost me. When I took the time to settle into my home, I realized I really enjoyed being there. When I acquired my third dog, Micah, my friend Peggy said, "Man, you don't plan on going anywhere ever again, do you?" I was known for taking off on a jaunt to Africa to visit my dad for three weeks at a time or some other exotic locale at the drop of a hat. But now I preferred to stick close to home. And guess what? When I stopped running around the world, the world came to me.

I discovered a new kind of wealth—the kind that can never go down in value—good

I believe one of the greatest measures in life of a rich character is not what you acquire but how you respond to loss and who you become in the midst of the test.

times, love, and laughter shared with those you love. It costs nothing to have a group of your nearest and dearest scream- ing over a game of Taboo or having a hearty discussion on how to solve the world's problems. Far too many times we choose expensive nights out to protect ourselves from getting as intimate as we should, to protect us from dealing with the real issues we struggle with. There is something about sitting at home in a good comfy chair that sets the atmosphere for deep exchanges, a communion of sorts, where you share from the heart. Sometimes it's the truth you don't even want to deal with, but there it is. It just spurted out over a cup of coffee along with your tears. But it is in those moments that you're glad you weren't anywhere else. You were safe. You were at home, and the advice you just got didn't cost you anything, and yet your spirit was enriched by the exchange. I believe one of the greatest measures in life of a rich character is not what you acquire but how you respond to loss and who you become in the midst of the test.

DIVA REFLECTIONS

Perhaps this whole thing about running out of money, cutting back, or whatever you want to call it, is more about rediscov- ering the other things we've lost along the way—like where our true wealth is hidden. Sometimes the basics aren't as flashy as the things we pride ourselves on acquiring, but in the end, the basic stuff is still there after you've lost everything else. And you know what? Getting back to the core of who you were before you left home, your base, is priceless.

WHAT'S A DIVA TO DO?

- Track yourself for a week. Keep a daily diary of all your activities—everything you do from pray to eat, where you went, and how long you were there.

- Now make an honest assessment of which things were necessary and which ones were just empty distractions and time robbers.

- Make a plan for which activities you need to purge from your list of things to do.

- Make a plan on how to be more disciplined with your time.

- Write your calendar for the week ahead of time, planning out your time. Include time for rest and play. This will help you own your time instead of time owning you.

26

CUT THE FAT

AN AMAZING THING happens when you stay at home. You discover all the things you have. Seriously, you discover the stuff you knew about and the stuff you didn't know about. The trouble with the stuff you don't know about is that you keep buying more because you either can't find what you're looking for or you don't know it's there.

George Carlin, the late comedian, once said that houses were big boxes for holding our stuff. When we get too much stuff, we tend to buy a bigger house to hold more stuff, but really, what we need to do is get rid of some of the stuff. At the end of the day, how much stuff do we need, and how much is it costing us? As I began my cleaning foray, I found all kinds of things. Why I needed three steam cleaners for my wood floors was beyond me. But again, the first one was tucked way in the back of a pantry closet and forgotten. The inventory of other duplicates I had was astonishing. So off they went to a corner to be photographed, cataloged, and posted on eBay. Not only did I make a tidy profit, but I felt soooo much better. I could think! Hoarding creates clutter, and physical disorder creates mental disarray, a lack of focus, and confusion. I truly believe that the way your house looks mirrors your spiritual condition. Disorder cannot be compartmentalized. I've experienced this personally. When my life and my spirit are in order, so is my home. If I feel off center, frazzled, and overwhelmed, my home reflects it.

I truly believe that the way your house looks mirrors your spiritual condition.

So now that I had cleared out the clutter and actually profited from it literally, I was ready to cut the fat in other areas that weren't so obvious. It was time to look at how I was bleeding money in other ways. First, I had to take a look at my utility bills. Where could I cut corners? Most utility companies have budget plans you can sign up for. They amortize your average and spread it out over the year to bring your monthly bill down. How many phones or phone plans do you have? I will add a note of caution here. Many people are using only a cell phone these days. However, it is recommended that you still have a landline in case of emergencies because cell phones are not always reliable. Why not check out a plan that offers you a bundle package deal on the landline, cell phone, and in many cases internet and cable television services? These packages can save you a bundle, thus the name, I guess. A great resource for comparing your long-distance costs is http://abtolls.com/compare/rateshome.html. You'll be able to find the best deals for your phone calling habits. Another option for long-distance and international calls is starting a Skype account online or using Yahoo! Messenger to make calls using your computer and a microphone for absolutely free! You can even do video messaging. Personally I don't feel like looking cute every time I make a call, so I just use the phone feature.

Make sure you are using energy-saving bulbs. A water filter can save you more in the long run if you are constantly buying bottles of water. Did you know that by reducing your shower by one minute, you will save a thousand gallons of water a year? If you put a quart-size milk jug in the tank of your toilet and fill it with water, it can displace ten gallons or more of water a day. This can save you on your water bill if you have one. How often do you do laundry? Even hotels are trying to cut back on doing laundry every day, thus the option you can now exercise to keep your towels and linens versus them being changed every day; using your towels more than once at home can cut down on the amount of laundry you have to do. Curtains can keep heat out when it's hot and warmth in when it's cold, and it's a beautiful way to save on heat and air-conditioning bills. It's not just cost efficient. It's energy efficient as well.

Beyond looking at your utilities to cut expenses, take stock of your refrigerator and pantry. How much food are you throwing away? I was totally guilty in this area. My eyes were too big for my stomach when I went to the grocery store. I always bought more than I could really consume. Food would sit in the refrigerator until it spoiled. I was throwing away more than I was consuming. I had to rethink how I purchased food. Now I make a concise list, and I don't buy more than I can consume in three to five days. My pared-down list saves me money.

There's something to be said for peace of mind and being realistic about what you can afford, not just financially, but emotionally and mentally as well.

Take a look at your other bills, too, to see where you may be able to make some changes. What about your cable bill? Do you really need cable television? I had to admit that I never got around to watching HBO and all the other extra channels I was paying for. Now you can watch most programs online absolutely free at your convenience! Want to watch a movie? For a small monthly fee, you select your movie choices to be mailed to you from Netflix or Blockbuster. (Under certain plans, if you return your Blockbuster movie to a Blockbuster store, you will receive a coupon for a free movie.)

Last but not least, consider downsizing, period. Perhaps the stress of a huge mortgage or pricey rental is not worth it in the long run. When I gave up my office to the bank, I found a rental that was twice the size and half the price of my mortgage. There's something to be said for peace of mind and being realistic about what you can afford, not just financially, but emotionally and mentally as well. Opt for something charming and small or another area of town that is not as expensive but chic in its own right.

Do you really need a car? Check out an I-GO car-share plan. Depending on your needs, you can sign up for a plan that ranges from nothing to thirty dollars a month. The only difference is the hourly charge and the mileage charge. But the fee includes gas and insurance. The bottom line? You can rake up massive savings if you don't need a car a lot and only use it for errands, etc. The other option is Zipcar, which basically operates the same way.

A well-kept or simply overlooked secret for buying cars at a lower price—buying your car from a car rental company! Most cars for sale only have ten- to forty-thousand miles on them and are in mint condition. Surprisingly, you can still finance, do a trade-in, and get extended warranties just like at the car dealership for way lower prices. I found the prices to be comparable if not less than car auctions for cars in better condition. Also check out swapalease.com for referrals to people looking for someone to take over their car leases. In some cases you could end up driving a car for free until the lease runs out. Some owners would rather pay off the lease than pay the fine for breaking the lease, therefore they need someone to maintain the car until the lease runs out.

Being honest and discerning between your wants and needs at home can save lots of money in the long run. The savings may not seem obvious right away, but the bottom line will reveal over time that the way to win the financial war is one step at a time, or literally one small reduction at a time.

DIVA REVELATION

True victory comes when you finally acknowledge that life does not consist of the things you own. Your possessions do not define you. Repeat after me: *I am not my house. The things I own neither add to nor detract from my value as a human being. They do not take away from what I have to offer to others. The things that are inherent to who I am as a person are the basis of my true wealth. Therefore I am not ruled by what I want or think I need. Life is bigger than that.* Yes, there is a difference between wealth and riches. Riches will come and go, but true wealth speaks to the quality of the life I've lived with or without many possessions. And that, my friend, is knowledge you can take to the bank.

WHAT'S A DIVA TO DO?

- Go over your utility bills with a fine-tooth comb and see where you can cut corners. When in doubt, call customer service and ask them how you can save on your bill.

- Be honest with yourself about what are unnecessary luxuries in your life right now.

- Get rid of the clutter!

- Have the courage to downsize if you need to.

- If you have something you don't need and someone else could use, give it up! Log onto freecycle.org to post what you want to give away. Craigslist.com also offers this under their free section. Someone will be happy to cart away your goodies. Remember, one man's trash is another man's, or woman's, treasure!

27

REDISCOVERING
THE KITCHEN

THE KITCHEN IS probably one of the most disdained yet powerful places in your house. It is the center of the home. Where does everyone gather at a party no matter what is going on elsewhere? The kitchen! It is the center of conversation and general lingering. It reminds us of home when we were little children. It was the place of comfort. Cookies were there and all the yummy delights that made us feel good. Now, fast-forward to adulthood. Mother is no longer there waiting to dole out all the delights that you never learned to cook, and the kitchen becomes the place we now avoid unless we're putting the leftovers in the refrigerator from a meal we ordered in. That is so wrong and so sad.

Not only do I think God is trying to get us all back to basics and community, but I think He's steering us back to the kitchen. The kitchen draws people together. It gets them to talk, to share, to nurture one another. There is something special about a home-cooked meal. There's a sense of completion for the person who cooked it and a feeling of significance for the one who eats it. Cooking is a sacrificial act of giving—of yourself, your time, and your resources. Personally, I love to cook—for other people. I don't like to cook for myself. But I had to approach cooking with a new attitude.

The kitchen draws people together. It gets them to talk, to share, to nurture one another.

As I tallied up how much I was spending eating out and ordering in, I could hear the kitchen calling me. "I wouldn't make you spend money like that. . . . Come back to me." And so I did. When I returned to my kitchen, I found that not only did I spend less money, but I ate in a more healthy fashion. I lost weight, I felt better, and I had more money. It was all so diva-licious!

Now that my weekly eating budget was reeled in and under control, I had to look at the other ways food had ruled my world and committed highway robbery. Since most holiday dinners and birthday celebrations were held at my house, I decided to take another approach to feeding the masses. You got it—a potluck buffet. Everyone was assigned a dish, and everyone was happy to oblige. They all came bearing their specialties. When it was all spread out, we had enough food to feed people for three days! It cost me a quarter of what I would have spent if I had prepared everything myself, and the food was doubly delicious. Everyone was invested in the meal and felt significant because they had made a contribution.

Recently, a friend of mine and I were trying to decide what we wanted to do for dinner. She said, "You know, I have vegetables I need to get rid of before I go out of town." I said, "I have some fish. Why don't I bring it over, and we can put something together for dinner." With that we had a wonderful dinner without spending a dime. We sat around the kitchen table, talking and laughing well into the night, and a waiter was not missed. Quality time doesn't have to cost an arm and a leg even if we are just talking chicken.

If you're not a good cook, there is an entire channel dedicated to teaching people how to cook (if you still have cable). The Food Network has programs that show you in detail how to prepare everything from a simple soup to a fancy dessert. Am I saying you should never eat out again? No. Absolutely not. But it should not be the norm for your week. Eating out should be the treat, not the staple. It just makes sense to control all the costs you can, and this is one of the easiest areas to reign right away.

Compare what you spend out to what that same amount spent at the grocery store would get you. The price of a salad could buy a whole head of lettuce, a couple of tomatoes, mushrooms. . . . You get the picture? The fifty dollars you spend at a restaurant is for one meal. The same fifty dollars buys enough groceries for several meals at home, depending on what you buy. But here again, you have to plan your work and work your plan. Make a realistic menu, and make some of your ingredients overlap to avoid having to throw away food.

One of the greatest investments I ever made was a Food-Saver. It seals food airtight in plastic sacks or special Food-Saver containers that keep things from getting freezer burn when you freeze them; it also keeps food from spoiling in the refrigerator. Waste not, want not. When we are resourceful with what we have, our dollars stretch further. Instead of tossing bananas that have gone soft, throw them in the blender with ice and some milk or juice and make a smoothie. It's called using what you have and being a wise steward of what you've been given. Think about it. If you're really serious about cutting all the unnecessary expenses from your life, then eating at home more makes more than just cents.

Waste not, want not. When we are resourceful with what we have, our dollars stretch further.

DIVA REVELATION

They say charity begins at home, and home is where the heart is. That being said, it suggests that home should be the place where you feel safest, nurtured, and secure. There is something to be said for breaking bread at your own table and sharing what you have with others. It's a coming together to feed one another—not just physically, but spiritually and emotionally as well. When the circumstances of life force us inward, don't view it as a sentence. See it as an opportunity to discover another facet of yourself that you can share with others. As some old habits die, you make room for a newness of life you could not imagine. Remember: no cocoon, no butterfly. Incubation always leads to sprouting wings that enable us to fly.

WHAT'S A DIVA TO DO?

- Pick up a copy of *Debt-Proof Living* by Mary Hunt for helpful tips. Log on to her Web site at debtproofliving.com for lots of ideas on how to save on household expenses.

- Do a comparison. Take your last restaurant check and make a list of what you could have bought at the grocery store for the same amount of money.

- Log on to coupons.com to find coupons for your groceries.

- Make sure you take advantage of cards associated with grocery stores for additional savings.

- Log on to the Internet and do a search for the type of recipes you want. There is an endless list available to you.

- Stick to your list, and don't overbuy.

28

MORE THAN ONE WAY TO SKIN A CHICKEN

OKAY, BEAR WITH ME on this experiment! I may not have a cooking show on the Food Network, but I'm going to show you a little something to get more out of your meals. Even if you're not a lover of leftovers, you can get more miles from your meals. Try doing more than one dish with a single item. Let's take chicken, for example. I came up with a way to get five meals out of one chicken. Mm-hmm. Now keep in mind, I am a single woman. However, this took major discipline on my part. Usually when I cooked, you would have thought I was preparing food for a small army. This was one of the ways I got in grocery trouble. I would fix these huge portions of food, and one of two things would happen: I'd either get sick of eating the same thing over and over again, or I'd put my leftover dish in the freezer and forget it was there until it got freezer burn and had to be thrown away. Sometimes I would have to get on the phone and find people to come over and eat all of the food I cooked. I always found willing takers, but I'm not a restaurant, okay? I had to master controlling my grocery budget but not feeling deprived. I needed to eat well but still have variety on a shoestring budget. Thus, my experiment: the five-meal chicken plan. I'll share my menu and recipes with you. Depending on the size of your household, you might have to double or triple the recipe and use two chickens instead of one.

Perhaps you can't control the circumstances of your financial meltdown, but there are some things you can control like how you respond to it and how you move forward from here.

Day One—Barbecue Chicken, Steamed Broccoli

Combine 3 tablespoons of soy sauce, ¾ cup of brown sugar, a pinch of dry mustard, 2 drops of Tabasco sauce, ⅛ cup of vinegar, ½ cup of barbecue sauce (I like Sweet Baby Ray's), 4 minced garlic cloves, ¼ cup of water, and 2 chicken bouillon cubes. Stir over medium heat for 5 minutes. This will make enough for you to store to use again over some salmon (or whatever you choose) the following week. Pour the sauce over a leg and a wing. Put chicken in the oven on 450 degrees for about 30 minutes. Steam your broccoli and have a delicious meal!

Day Two—Chicken with Sautéed Spinach

Take a leg, wing, and ½ breast, and season with a touch of salt and pepper; rub with a little garlic, and pour Italian dressing over them. Put in fridge overnight to marinate. Next day, bake meat in the oven at 375 degrees for 30 minutes or until golden brown. Sautée spinach until bright green, approximately 5-7 minutes. Put the breast away for the next day.

Day Three— Grilled Chicken Salad

Take the chicken breast from the day before. You can either heat it or eat it cold. Slice it into strips. Make a salad with lettuce, mushrooms, red pepper, mandarin orange slices, cucumber, grape tomatoes, and almond slivers. Place the chicken breast on top for a yummy mélange of flavors kissing your tongue without adding anything to your hips.

Day Four—Chicken Salad

Take the other chicken breast, season it, and steam. Cut it up into cubes along with some sweet onion and some seedless grapes—as much as you would like. Add mayo and a dash of mustard, according to the consistency you desire. Place your mixture on top of a bed of lettuce for a refreshing light lunch or dinner.

Day Five—Chicken Soup

You are now left with the back of the chicken. Season and steam the back of the chicken along with ½ onion and 1 tomato. Allow the onion and tomato to get tender. Put the tomato and onion in a blender and liquefy. Pour over chicken and add ½ teaspoon dried red pepper, ½ cup chicken stock, or 1 bouillon cube and a cup of water, a dash of pepper and simmer. If you like, you can add a cubed potato and a vegetable. If you want a more tomato-tasting base, add a tablespoon of tomato paste. Add a side salad, and you've got a tasty meal that will leave you satisfied but not in pain.

Perhaps you are not into chicken. You can do the same thing with any of your meat choices or tofu. It's not so much the recipes but the principle behind it—be resourceful. Don't give in to waste. Use everything you have, and get the most that you can out of it. As you stretch your resources, your savings will increase and produce great dividends for you. This is a good exercise because if you are easily bored like me, variety is truly the spice of life for you. In order for you to remain disciplined, the choices you make still have to be enjoyable. If in any way you give in to feeling deprived, you will binge and spend money you can't afford to part with. So be creative, and bon appétit!

As you stretch your resources, your savings will increase and produce great dividends for you.

DIVA REVELATION

Planning your meals does more than give you a terrific menu; it also makes you aware of what you are eating. This is one of the keys to weight loss and maintaining your diet. In times of stress, many resort to comfort food and unconsciously eat whatever makes them feel good in the moment, which can result in more pounds. This can only serve to acerbate an even greater problem. Now you've got to buy new clothes. Another expense you don't need! When you are going through financial stress, discipline must be exercised on all fronts. From the way you spend your money, to what you eat, to what you buy. It is all tied together. Perhaps you can't control the circumstances of your financial meltdown, but there are some things you can control, such as how you respond to it and how you move forward from here.

WHAT'S A DIVA TO DO?

- Make a list of your favorite meals. Take note of the similar components.

- Build your menu around those ingredients, then shop for what you need to add to what you already have.

- Be creative, experiment with recipes, and find new ways to eat your old favorites.

- Invite a friend over and cook together. Exchange recipes and even dishes.

- At work, have a food pool. Have everyone bring one ingredient to make a huge salad or meal for lunch. This way everyone only pays for one ingredient, and you end up with a feast!

29

WALMART, TAR-JAY, AND OTHER EXOTIC LOCALES

I HEARD A PREACHER once say that whenever he wanted to be romantic with his wife, he took her to Walmart. This put her in the mood for romance. I know what he means. When everyone else started screaming about Walmart and Target stores years ago, I wondered what all the fuss was about. Then I went and found out. Oh my, it was a veritable feast of all things at prices I couldn't believe! From clothing to household goods, it was like going on a treasure hunt. Every aisle had its own wonderful finds.

Recently I found out that Walmart carried one of my

favorite designers. Yes, it's true! I had traveled to New York on business and decided to stop by Norma Kamali's store. Imagine my surprise to see her window filled with items that ranged from nine to twenty dollars. Going inside to investigate further, we spotted Norma Kamali herself!

Just because you don't have a lot of money doesn't mean your home can't be beautiful.

"Norma!" I said, to which she said, "I remember you. You're Michelle Hammond, right?" You could have knocked me over with a feather; we had met several years before. After we got past the celebration of her remembrance, she informed me that her window display was in celebration of debuting her line of clothing for Walmart. My friend Valencia and I lost our minds. One hundred dollars later, I was too chic for myself. But back to household stuff.

Whatever your household, beauty, and even wardrobe needs are, they can be found at Walmart, or *Tar-Jay*, as many have called Target. Let's not leave Costco, Kohl's, and Sam's Club out of the equation. Oh, the wonder of it all! Many of these stores are superstores that can cover pretty much all of your needs, even gas for your car! You've got to love it. Because they buy in bulk and, in some cases, sell in bulk, you can experience major savings. One of my favorite lines of cleaners is Method. Nontoxic and biodegradable, Method brand products are quality products for cleaning everything from hands, to glass, to furniture beautifully. In places like Walmart, Method offers a cleaning kit, which includes several products that you can purchase for the same price as what one cleanser could cost alone.

These stores are a haven for those searching for knickknacks for home—cute pillows, glassware, some furnishings. You can get lost wandering the aisles. I must caution you to exercise self-control and stick to your list when you visit one of these superstores. Why? Because beyond the household sections, there are beauty products, clothing, groceries in some cases, even a rack where you are sure to find one of my books! Yes, girl, it is all there. Prescriptions, glasses, contacts . . . shall I go on?

Were you a Williams-Sonoma kind of girl in better financial days? No need to fear, Bed Bath & Beyond beckons with all sorts of gadgets to set the kitchen diva in you free. They also have curtains, towels, bedding, beautiful ensembles for your bathroom . . . you name it. Just because you don't have a lot of money doesn't mean your home can't be beautiful. Stores like these have put a beautiful home within reach at prices you can afford.

Sometimes it takes learning from our mistakes and learning during the lean times to really make a lesson stick.

Marshalls is another good one for things for the home. I always go there to get things like picture frames, candles, decorative items, and of course, the occasional good bargain on clothing.

Okay, so here's my breakdown: Costco or Sam's Club for all my paper goods and laundry stuff. That's a trip I can make about every two months unless I return with my shopping club to bulk-food shop or to shop for a party. Here is where you can find shrimp platters, sushi plates, fruit and veggie platters, and tons of frozen hors d'oeuvres for far less than you would pay for them at a regular grocery store—and they are delicious. I laid out a spread for thirty people for under one hundred dollars. Anytime you need larger quantities, your superstore clubs are the place.

Walmart and Target are great for household miscellaneous things as well as personal hygiene items. They also have great pet supplies. If I don't go online to Doctors Foster and Smith or go to Petco, I head straight for Walmart and Target. They have a great supply of food and creature comforts. I was pleasantly surprised to find great underwear at both of these stores, too, for ridiculously low prices. I found out what Victoria's Secret was—there are more reasonably priced bras and panties somewhere else! Kohl's also has great underwear, and who can forget that they carry Vera Wang fashions?! Hey, I didn't say you couldn't shop. I'm just asking you to watch what you're spending and where you're spending.

It's amazing how we fool ourselves into thinking we have progressed by being able to shop at "higher end" stores. Do you really just like throwing money away? That's exactly what you're doing if you're spending money that you don't have to.

Every penny saved adds up to less stress for you as your savings grow and you have a cushion for hard times when they come. Notice I said *when*, not *if*, hard times come. Hard times will come in every life. It is inevitable. Most people who have acquired great wealth lost a whole lot of money before they got rich. Some have lost and regained their wealth several times. This is where the priceless lessons are learned on what is truly valuable. People always say you should use your common sense, but sense is not common. Sometimes it takes learning from our mistakes and learning during the lean times to really make a lesson stick. This is where you learn wisdom about how to handle money. You learn to become a careful spender, a more thoughtful and prudent consumer. In the thirty-first chapter of Proverbs, one of my favorite books of the Bible, there's a line that always struck me in the description of the virtuous woman. It says that she doesn't worry about tomorrow.[1] She's prepared for whatever occurs. She's confident that she will have whatever she needs. This security comes not only from planning but from walking circumspectly every day. It's about not just living in the moment but also having as much of a plan as one can have for tomorrow. Even the creatures in nature prepare for the winter. They save. How much more should we? It's time to wise up, sister, and cut corners where you can. You can't afford not to.

DIVA REVELATION

It's not where you shop; it's what you buy and how much you spend. When you've acquired good staples in life—a few quality pieces such as a good black dress, one nice piece of jewelry—you know, the investment pieces that should last through every trend—inexpensive pieces look just as expensive when coordinated with what you already have. Disposable items are just that—disposable. They are not worth spending a lot of money on. It's time to stop spending money just because—it eventually leads to where you are right now. Someone once said that God gave us two ears and one mouth so we would listen more than we spoke, have more input than output. The same is true with our finances. We should have more input than output. So get creative. Find the joy in saving, and save the extravagance for giving (and spending) where it matters.

WHAT'S A DIVA TO DO?

- Do a search for discount and wholesale stores in your area. Take a day to go and discover what is available to you so you know where to find it.

- Discover the world of online. You can literally put the word *wholesale* and whatever you're looking for in your search engine for a list of sources to buy whatever you want at reduced costs. (For example, wholesale electronics or wholesale baby items will give you a list of sites that allow you to find electronics or baby items at a fraction of the original cost.)

- Join a warehouse—split the membership with a friend if you must. The cost of membership will pay for itself in light of all that you will save.

- Promise yourself you will never spend more than you have to, and stick to the promise.

- Decide that, for everything you buy in excess, you have to give something away until you break the habit.

30

KEEP THE FAITH

AS I WRITE THIS CHAPTER, I still don't really know the entire outcome of my financial situation. I don't know if I'll be able to keep my home. I am still making a list of adjustments and checking them twice. But I have peace in the midst of the storm. Yesterday at church I stood talking to a man who had a real estate development company. He told me he had lost everything. His business was shut down, and he was rewriting his résumé to look for work for the first time in twenty-five years. I related my own list of challenges, he nodded understandingly, and we both said at the same time, "But God is faithful." It was a quiet conversation with very real concerns shared. With no hint of pride or urgency, we admitted it was a scary time. But we were also quick to summarize that, though we did not know what tomorrow held for us, we did know Who held tomorrow, and that was very comforting.

If you're listening to the news all the time, you will be consumed by fear. But as we look to God, His conversation is very different.

The other day I celebrated paying off a few credit cards and paying down others halfway. A few days later, I received a notice that they had lowered my limit to an amount slightly below what I had paid and then charged me a forty-dollar over-the-limit fee for a new limit I had not been informed I had! My church member and I shared how creditors and banks were making it difficult for people to do the right thing. As fear grips everyone, people become more desperate, more hard of heart, less gracious—just downright mean. Small wonder, the Bible says that faith comes by hearing—so think about what we're hearing.[1] If you're listening to the news all the time, you will be consumed by fear. But as we look to God, His conversation is very different. He promises to supply all of our needs according to *His* riches, not the world's banking system.[2] They may not be the wants we had on our lists, but He is consistent in giving us what we truly need. I focus on finding rest in that.

As I've taken two steps forward and five steps back in some instances, there have been times I've felt I was drowning in my debt. Sometimes no matter what I do, I fail to see the light at the end of the tunnel, although I know it's there. For a brief moment in the midst of my struggles, I've understood why some have given up, clocked out, jumped out of windows, sought to escape the process of recovery. In those moments, the only thing that has not allowed me to follow suit is the confidence that God is able to supply streams in the desert and cause me to flourish in the midst of famine if I hold fast and wait on Him.

You might ask, *Well, Michelle, if you trust God so much, then why would He let you go through this?* All I can say is that I believe God loves me enough to let me go through it to bring me to a better place—a place where He can trust me with much more than what He has already given me. It's part of the process of becoming. I have to confess my own sins: I'm good at making money, but I have also abused it, not handled it wisely, and basked in ignorance for a long time. You see, sin isn't always about the stuff that sets the world's hair on fire. It may not be as blatant as murder or anything like that. Sometimes it's the little foxes that ruin the vines. It's the little sins that destroy us and damage our security, our peace of mind, and our well-being. These are just as awful to God because He so longs for us to experience not just a right standing with Him, but joy, peace, and fulfillment in our everyday living. When we experience victory in our lives, it makes Him look good. It glorifies Him. That's when He smiles His brightest smile. Our pleasure gives Him pleasure.

As I consider the encouragement the Word of God gives for hard times, I see what God is up to, and that makes me relax and allow Him to finish what He has begun in me.

Quiet as it is kept, ignorance is not bliss. God says His people perish for lack of knowledge.[3] I have learned more about money and ways to save since I've had my financial fallout than in all the years I was basking in plenty. Why? Because I had to in order to make it through. God is determined not to leave us in the condition He found us in. And so He allows the circumstances of life to correct and discipline us. He is so determined to bring us to full maturity that He allows suffering to do its work. The testing of our faith produces perseverance. Or as *The Message* version of the Bible says in the book of James, we should "consider it a sheer gift . . . when tests and challenges come at [us] from all sides." Because "under pressure, [our] faith-life is forced into the open and shows its true colors." The author goes on to suggest that we shouldn't "try to get out of anything prematurely." We should let our trials "do [their] work so [that we can] become mature and well-developed, not deficient in any way."[4] I believe God can deliver me from anything, but I don't presume that He will. Only He knows if the things I desire will make or break me. I know that He will allow me to suffer whatever I need to in order to refine me.

As I consider the encouragement the Word of God gives for hard times, I see what God is up to, and that makes me relax and allow Him to finish what He has begun in me. We are encouraged to endure hardship as a form of discipline. God understands that discipline does not feel good and can even be dreadfully painful, but He also promises that we come out the better for it. Discipline and hardship actually train us and produce great peace and righteousness when the process is completed. As a matter of fact, the apostle Paul explains in the book of Romans that suffering not only produces perseverance, but it tempers us and produces sound character and an even stronger hope in what God will do next in our lives.[5] We've learned from experience that He always comes through for us; we have a running track record of past deliverances.

So what does that mean for me? It means I keep slugging away at what seems to be a mountain of debt. It means I don't grow discouraged in the moments when it doesn't feel as if I'm making progress. It means that I do all that I can do and leave the rest to God. In the meantime, I don't let my trials change me for the worse. I continue to give, to have a generous heart, to have hope and remain grateful.

Life can change so quickly, you have to leave room for God to surprise you. And I just love surprises, don't you?

DIVA REVELATION

I have learned more about myself during this period of lack than any other time—my vulnerabilities, the things I needed to correct in my thinking. I've discovered some misguided values that needed to be redirected. It has been a liberating time. I told a friend recently, "Perhaps I'm too exhausted to get excited about anything anymore." But the truth of the matter is that trials put life in perspective. Loss does the same thing. When you get to the place where you have nothing left to lose, you are able to release everything. You find the victory in transparency and the letting go of the things you once clung to. None of it is really ours, anyway. It all belongs to God. It is simply on loan to us. What we do with what we are given determines how much more we get. Sometimes the blessing of the Lord doesn't make us rich in the way we would like it to, but it does make us develop a wealth of character. At the end of the day when you leave this earth, no one is going to discuss your finances and what you owned; they are going to talk about the type of person you were and how you affected others.

WHAT'S A DIVA TO DO?

- Examine the foundation of your faith and what you believe.

- Search for God's promises to you in His Word, and choose to personalize them. Write them down, repeat them, pray them until they take root in your soul and feed your faith.

- Keep moving forward.

- Do what you can do, and leave the rest to God.

- Don't give up.

- Always be grateful.

31

ASK DADDY

I SAT LOOKING AT THE PHONE, wondering if I could really press past my pride to call my father and ask for help. This would be the second time he had to bail me out of financial trouble. I couldn't do it again. I didn't think I could bear to be lectured or questioned about why I couldn't get my act together. I was too old to be calling home, I said to myself; my father would be disappointed in me, in the fact that I had not been able to take care of myself. The constant urgings of my closest friends finally made me decide to call. "What have you got to lose?" they said. All he could say was no when I asked, I finally resolved. Like Queen Esther going before the king of Persia, I adopted an "if I perish, I perish" attitude.[1]

When I called my father, I opted for quietly relaying the facts of my predicament. No tears or hysteria like the first time. He calmly asked how much I needed. I told him. It was no small amount. He calmly sighed and said, "Alright, I will take care of it." Just like that. No questions, no lectures. No bringing up the last time. I don't know why I expected to be berated. After all, he is my father, my daddy. I was supposed to be able to crawl into his lap and share everything that was in my heart—my fears, my concerns, my questions—and find comfort and answers in his presence. No matter how old I was, I was still his child. He was still committed to taking care of me, protecting me, counseling me, loving me. Why, then, did I expect the worst?

I sat thinking about how that same attitude went beyond my earthly father to my heavenly Father. One part of my brain told me that my heavenly Father was generous and loving. Another part of my brain feared God's displeasure. I feared His rebuke for not getting it right and being subjected to yet another hard lesson until I did. I am not of the opinion that life with God means smooth sailing. I am cognizant of the fact that the only thing that separates believers from unbelievers is how we go through the process of becoming—how we handle trial and upset, what guides our decisions, choices, and principles. But the long and short of it is, it rains on the just and the unjust.[2] In His infinite fairness, God does not shield us from the rain, but He does wash us with it. He clears a path for us to walk through the storm and safely ushers us to the other side of every trial. There He dries our tears and whispers encouragement and reassurances.

The Father knows the way I take. He also knows my makeup. He knows how much I can bear as well as what it takes for me to grow into the person He knows I will become. He is relentless in His pursuit of the best in all of us. And so He allows us to be shaken and pressed until we yield to His touch completely. With our submission comes a beauty and a peace that can never be stolen, no matter what occurs in our lives. In the midst of it all, somehow, someway, we make it through and emerge the better for it.

In Psalms, David said he had never seen the righteous forsaken or their children begging bread.[3] And when I look over my situation, no matter what I've thought I lacked, there are some things I must acknowledge: I still have a roof over my head. I still eat every day. I still have a sound mind and a healthy body. A lady at a women's conference I attended recently said, "There are ten things you need to thank God for every morning. One—He woke you up this morning. Two—He woke you up this morning. Three—He woke you up this morning. Four . . ." (You get the picture.) Things can always be worse. As long as you have breath and God has claimed you as His child, there is hope for your life, and you can know with confidence that all is not lost. Therefore, you can rest assured that He is approachable. He will not chastise you or fuss at you for coming or even for failing—if that is the case. He is faithful to love you and provide for you.

Rehearse what [God] has done for you in the past, and anticipate what He is going to do for you in the future.

Therefore, decide to wait passionately on your Abba Father. And while you wait, nurture a heart of gratitude. Rehearse what He has done for you in the past and anticipate what He is going to do for you in the future. I realized that the only thing that disappointed my daddy was my lack of faith in him. Though he wanted my respect, he did not want me to see him as unapproachable. He anticipated and waited for me to give him opportunities to be my hero. Instead, I thought my independence would impress him, but that was the last thing he wanted. Though he wanted me to thrive, he needed to be needed by me as well.

Need can be a beautiful thing that leads us to hidden treasures we didn't know existed—like the stuff that really matters.

My dependence on him was a source of connection that warmed his heart. He loved it when I was still his "little girl." I could say the same for my heavenly Father.

Wow! The world has fooled us into thinking that true strength is found in not needing anyone, being independent. Yet God says in *The Message* version of Psalm 91 that "if you'll hold on to [Him] for dear life . . . [He'll] get you out of any trouble. [He'll] give you the best of care if you'll only get to know and trust [Him]."[4] He invites us to call Him, and He will answer and be by our side in bad times. God invites us to depend on Him. He sees no shame in that, only an opportunity for Him to show up and be our Daddy, our Jehovah-Jireh, our Provider. And as He provides for us, we, in turn, can reach out to a brother or sister in need and share what we have. It is not what we accumulate that unites us; it is what we lack. Need can be a beautiful thing that leads us to hidden treasures we didn't know existed—like the stuff that really matters.

DIVA REVELATION

Job said that the Lord gives and the Lord takes away, but I don't believe that.[5] I think the Lord gives and we drop the ball. And He keeps picking it back up and giving it back to us until we are able to hold it. After all, that's what every loving father does with his children. The only one who is truly disappointed in us is us—sometimes we are our worst enemies, cutting off our noses to spite our faces. We jump to conclusions that can rob us of a blessing. The last frontier to receiving blessings is overcoming pride and simply asking for what we need. When we do, the windows of heaven open, and we see God at His finest. We see Him as the Father He promised to be. Our prayers may not be answered in the way we ask for Him to answer, but He will answer in a way that will bless us and meet our needs in unexpected ways. Sometimes He shows off all by Himself and works a miracle that you can't deny. Sometimes He uses others that you wouldn't expect, so be open. Remember, you can't have a testimony without first having a test!

WHAT'S A DIVA TO DO?

- Get over yourself.

- Talk to your Papa God.

- Be open to sharing with others who may be able to help you.

32

RECEIVE WHAT
YOU BELIEVE

I STARTED THIS BOOK off by saying that we were dealing with a redefined meaning of diva, not the world's definition. D.I.V.A. is my acronym for Divine Inspiration for Victorious Attitude. Attitude is everything, especially when you are going through the rough places in life. I am not a financial analyst, but I can tell you that many who know all the facts and figures have fallen in times of lack because their attitudes dictated that they could not handle life without the material items they were used to having. Fear overwhelmed them as they looked at their losses and concluded that life was no longer worth living. Some have killed themselves, leaving a family and friends reeling in the aftermath. Some have taken their families out with them, deciding everyone was better off dead.

It saddens me that some people would believe that their possessions and bank accounts were so much a part of who they were. Outside of what they owned, they had no identity, no significance; therefore, they ended their existence without considering how that would affect those they loved. To them, nothing mattered more than what had been lost, which is the biggest deception in the world.

What do you believe about where you are right now? It will affect all of your tomorrows. I remember that, when I first shared with my intimate circle of friends the state of my affairs, not one of them blinked. They looked at me and said, "Well, we can't wait to see what is going to happen in your life. Every time you have a setback, you always emerge heads and tails above where you fell. Think about it, Michelle. Every time there has been a crisis, it's been a setup for something amazing to come out of it all!" They began going down the list—rehearsing the amazing rebounds one after the other. "I'm sorry," one of my friends said. "I can't feel sorry for you, because I know I'm going to be jealous in a minute. Just wait and see!" Even if I had wanted to descend into the pit of depression, no one would allow me to go there. It was not conducive to victory.

Depression, apathy, resignation, anger, frustration . . . they all paralyze you. If God was trying to give you a new idea and creative invention to get you out of your situation, you wouldn't be able to receive it or believe it. Tell the truth, and shame the devil. You have to get a new attitude about your situation.

Here is a classic example of how the wrong attitude can be your undoing. The announcement has been made on every news station. The economy has tanked. It's the worst it's ever been. We're in a recession . . . no, a depression . . . blah, blah, blah. . . . So what does everybody do? Stop spending money, which drives us further aground. Thanks a lot to all the fearmongers. It's working. But remember, fear is simply False Evidence Appearing Real. Let's face it: Aliens did not come down from outer space and suck up all the money. It's still here. Some people are still flourishing. Therefore, we just have to find where the money is. Look for new streams—new streams of income and provision.

If I settle into the belief that there is no hope for me financially, I will just stop dead in my tracks, give up, and get no further. I cannot give in to my emotions.

If I settle into the belief that there is no hope for me financially, I will just stop dead in my tracks, give up, and get no further. I cannot give in to my emotions. My decisions must drive my emotions, not the other way around. Like the lepers who pondered their fate during a famine in the Bible in 2 Kings 7:3-11, we all must consider our options and dare to think outside the box. The lepers considered the possibilities before them. They decided they could stay where they were and die (at the entrance of the city), or go into the city and die (where the famine was), or take their chances with turning themselves in to the enemy's camp (where they could be fed or killed). Either they would eat and live or die. So they headed toward the camp and found it completely deserted with all the enemy's loot and provisions left behind. They ate, drank, and carried off silver, gold, and clothing. After they had collected enough for themselves, they went to the besieged city to report their findings, and everyone went out and shared in the wealth.

Every day we get to choose if we will live or die, wither or flourish. The choice is up to us. Choose not to be mastered by your circumstances, but rather master your response. Your response will affect the way others respond to you and supply you with the favor you need to make it through. Whether it's through financial or other tangible ways of support and help, your attitude will attract all you need to press past where you are right now.

Choose not to be mastered by your circumstances, but rather master your response.

So do an attitude check. Have you been so angry with God that you haven't spoken to Him? Well, how will you get instruction from Him if you've cut Him off? Are you seeing others as the source of your problems? Have you cut yourself off from the very ones who may be able to help you? How can you gain grace and patience from them if you're not cooperating or communicating?

When we decide to be a victor and not a victim, our entire posture changes the way we approach things. When I am walking in the confidence that I know God has my back, I can be bold enough to ask for what I want. After all, you have not because you ask not, right? But if I lack confidence in any part of my journey, I will fold and not move forward. I become my own worst enemy because what I believe becomes my greatest hindrance to victory.

What should you believe? First of all, that there is hope; every setback is a setup for a better view, a greater opportunity. It is only when we grow uncomfortable that we consider other options. As they say, when one door closes, open a window and get a different view. When the phone calls slowed for speaking engagements, I decided to create my own thing and take it around the country. I had no choice. I could relate to the lepers. Why stay home and die? So off I go. If I die, I will die trying. But I don't believe that will be the case. My attitude is simply this: I have everything within me that I need to make it in this world, and with the help of God, I will. And so will you.

Instead of looking at the mess life has made around you, own your stuff, take responsibility for your part in your mess, and decide you have an amazing opportunity to experience something you would not have experienced in your previous state of comfort: getting to witness a real-life success story right before your eyes—yours.

DIVA REVELATION

Trite but true, life is what you make it. It starts with faith, is driven by attitude, and is resolved by your actions. Since faith without works is dead, you've got to do something. I believe this is why a lot of folk don't like to pray. Because if you truly pray as you should, God is going to answer you. He is going to give you something to do. Life is a partnership with Him. He does His part, but it only works when you do your part.

Your part is simple. Keep the right attitude, use what He gives you, and do what He says. Little becomes much if you stay on track and don't give up; and you'll only give up if you believe there is no hope. So you'd better talk to yourself until you believe what you are saying! As David said, "Soul, why art thou so downcast? Trust in God!"[1]

WHAT'S A DIVA TO DO?

- Find the promises of God in the Word that relate to your situation. Post them where you can see them. Memorize them. Get them down in your spirit. Act like you believe them until you do.

- Face your fears and put them to rest. You are not your yesterday, and tomorrow holds endless options.

- Choose to make an action plan for yourself, and stick to it no matter what.

- Believe that people will help you, and ask for help.

- Keep hope alive.

33

HOW TO LIVE IN A HOUSE THAT'S BEYOND YOUR MEANS

WHILE ANTICIPATING the very real concern that I might lose my home, I began weighing what my other options might be. There were a few things I had learned that I wish someone had told me before becoming a proud but naive home owner. I had spent so many years happily renting that when others were chiding me to buy a home, I was in no hurry whatsoever. I never stopped to really think about what was important to me. Knowing what your lifestyle requires has everything to do with whether home ownership is for you. In my case, it was probably not the best idea, though my experience may have tainted my outlook.

When you are renting, you get all the benefits without the responsibility of owning a home. Something broken? Call the building engineer. Something wrong with the building? The cost of your rent is not affected. It's a beautiful thing! Travel a lot? If the building has a doorman or security, you feel safe. Your home is within secure confines. It's kind of like living in a hotel—depending on the quality of the staff. The last building I rented in had indoor parking with a valet that parked your car and brought it down when you called. It also had an on-the-premises cleaners. I was in hog heaven. I had found the place at a steal of a deal and stayed there for nine years without major rent increases. The building engineer's wife looked out for me when I was away on trips, collecting my mail and putting it inside my apartment. . . . Ah, I get nostalgic just thinking about it; life was so simple then.

Knowing what your lifestyle requires has everything to do with if home ownership is for you.

Now, fast-forward to me growing up and getting my own home. The excitement of new construction and the ability to pick everything I wanted from the tile to the floors wore off quickly when we discovered that the developer hadn't tuck-pointed the building or done the roof properly. You guessed it. I and everyone who owned in the building had to pay a special assessment, which came up to a staggering thirty thousand dollars (that was my part!). That's like a down payment on another house! In the midst of my financial crisis, that special assessment on top of the basic assessments that had magically more than tripled in a matter of six years became the bane of my existence. On top of that, my mortgage had doubled from refinancing on an adjustable rate that ballooned before I could refinance again. I was paying for what could have amounted to another apartment, and it hurt. No, make that several comfortable apartments.

So there I sat, weighing my financial options. In the middle of a market where my property was upside down, I decided that perhaps it was a better idea for me to cut my losses and get out. Where would I go? I decided to go back to renting until I could recoup. As I priced things around me, I found that I could live in a very nice place for a third of what I was presently paying. There was no shame in that. I considered it wise stewardship. Presently, I felt I was throwing a ton of money into a black hole. After almost being evicted for back assessments, I was no longer feeling the love for my home or surroundings. I felt violated. The complaints against the board from fellow neighbors only confirmed this was not the experience I wanted to continue having.

As I drifted down the street, my eyes fell on this beautiful mansion. I had lusted after it on many occasions. I had practically watched it being built. But today was the first day that I realized it had been sitting vacant for over a year. There was a lonely and rather dilapidated For Sale sign swinging in the breeze as if to say, "Why doesn't anybody want me? I'm so fabulous. . . . " "Yeah," I sighed, "Fabulous and run down." The yard was terribly neglected, and the house itself, though beautiful, looked deserted, dark, and scary. I remembered that an athlete had lived in the house. He had been robbed in it and moved out. Since then he had moved out of state to play, put the house up for sale, and left the house standing there all alone with no takers.

I thought to myself, *I could live in that house. He should let me house-sit that house for him.* I didn't even know his name. A friend of mine lived in the mansion across the alley from him, so I called her to find out if she knew him or how to contact him. She knew who he was but didn't have any way of reaching him. I continued pondering how I could find him. Suddenly I sat up in the seat and said, "Wait a minute! God, you know who this guy is. You know who knows him. If this is not a cockamamy idea, you can put that person in front of me!"

And half an hour later—I kid you not—I was talking to a young lady who was going on and on about how one of my books had changed her life and helped her in her relationship with the athlete she was dating. I stopped and asked her if she knew anything about this guy I was trying to find. She stopped and blurted out the guy's name! I was dumbfounded. "You know him?" I asked. "Oh, yeah!" she exclaimed. "His cousin and I are really close; we hang out together all the time." Next thing I knew, I was on the phone with the guy.

I told him I was interested in renting his home and keeping it up while it was on the market. I knew anything that expensive was not going to sell for a year or two, which would give me time to recoup. It could help him keep the house looking good and perhaps at least pay his taxes. He was interested. I submitted a written proposal with all the conditions and awaited his reply. Unfortunately, his deal was not renewed, and he moved back into the house.

But this led to a whole new way of thinking for me. I mentioned bartering in an earlier chapter; well, that is not limited to services and items. You can work out deals with housing, too! I was sharing this story with a realtor friend of mine who then chirped happily, "Oh yes, you could be a home manager for a show home!" She went on to tell me that there are companies that either hire people to live in mansions and other high-end homes or allow them to live there for a fraction of the cost. One news report showed this guy living in a three-million-dollar mansion for twelve hundred dollars a month! The responsibility of the home manager is to furnish and decorate the place (they give you assistance on this) and keep it clean and showable. That's it! You can log on to showhomes.com for more info on this.

The caveat, of course, is that, if the house sells, you have to move again, but they find another home to put you in. Talk about living like a queen for a mere pittance! For me, the houses I looked up were not in convenient locations for me, but depending on where you are, it could just work out to be above and beyond your dreams.

But the adventure didn't stop there. As I began looking around for rentals, I found another apartment that I really liked. However, there were a few things that I felt needed to be fixed in order to make it more desirable. The realtor had even commented on the fact that she didn't understand why it wasn't rented out yet. I knew why. There were some wiring and kitchen issues and a bad paint job.

After acquiring an estimate of what it would cost to address these needs, I asked her to ask the owners if they would be willing to waive the deposit and three months' rent in exchange for me fixing these things. I showed them photos of my home, and they were so impressed they said yes! This would afford me the luxury of not having to pull together the initial money that would have been required for me to move. It was a win-win for everyone involved. They would get an upgraded apartment back when I moved out, and it gave me time to address the things I told them I would fix at my own leisure since I would have the length of my rental agreement to accomplish my redecorating. At this time, we are still working out some minor details and I'm trying to sell my condo, but it looks like the rental deal will work out!

At this point, the world is your oyster if you are willing to be creative when it comes to how to acquire living space. There is something to be learned from every experience. Should I buy again, I will buy a house or a townhome that has no board or assessments, not a condo. When it's all yours, at least if you spend money, it's your choice. You can hire a handyman service to do what a building engineer does if you're single and not gifted with handyman skills. If I ever bought a condominium again, which is a very distant "if," it would have to be an older, established building with a large reserve to stave off surprise assessments. Though they can't be avoided, they can be a little more controlled than a newer building with no stash for emergencies and major repairs. In tandem with surprise fees is the feeling that though you own your home, you are still subject to other peoples' rules and decisions on what to do with the building you live in. Not cool in some instances. If I own my home, I should be able to have ten dogs if I want to or put a rug in the hallway, if you get my drift. Looking back, the money I could have saved if I had continued renting would have kept me out of the mess I'm presently in. But that is neither here nor there. It is simply an expensive lesson. You live, you learn, and you find someplace cuter to lay your head down in peace while embracing the awesome privilege of being able to begin again.

If home is where the heart is, make sure your heart feels safe; find peace over profit or debt.

If home is where the heart is, make sure your heart feels safe; find peace over profit or debt. Remember that there are many ways to get the home of your dreams without it depleting you financially or emotionally.

So there you have it. House-sitting is a fabulous option, as well as bartering redecorating for months off your rent. Not too shabby, huh? Perhaps the greater moral to this story is what necessity forces you to discover. When the going gets tough, the tough get creative. Here's to happy house hunting!

DIVA REVELATION

Your home is definitely the center of your heart. It is the one oasis in the middle of the storms of life, or at least it should be. Though your home does not define who you are, it can affect you, so choose your situation wisely. I believe a house holds more than just your stuff. It holds precious moments and memories that will be with you for a lifetime, so make room for those things without allowing it to cost you something even more priceless—your joy.

WHAT'S A DIVA TO DO?

- Write a list of what is important to you to maintain your quality of life.

- Decide which situation best fits your lifestyle choices—renting or owning.

- Investigate thoroughly before purchasing a home or condo. You can Google the address you are considering. In some instances, past owners and tenants will leave reviews of their living experiences there.

- Find out the financials and the reserves of a condo building. Make sure you do a thorough inspection of a home before committing.

- Don't be afraid to offer terms to your potential landlord that would benefit you both.

- Check out all your housing options. Rentals, foreclosures, or house-sitting—the market is wide open. There are more privately owned apartments for rent than ever. Private owners tend to be more lenient if you have bad credit than large management companies.

34

FINAL DIVA THOUGHTS

LIKE I ALWAYS SAY, I may be down, but I'm not out. Hopefully my simple approach to keeping your head above water and keeping your spirit intact will give you the impetus to put one foot in front of the other until you get to the other side of your lack or setback. Then I highly recommend, when you are back in the chips, that you seek the counsel of those who know all that deep, technical stuff about bonds, trusts, savings, portfolios, and the like. As a matter of fact, study up while you are still broke so that you'll be ready. On second thought, get a head start now. It's never too late to start or begin to recover what you lost. Your tomorrow begins today.

So decide to put away childish habits and mind-sets that keep you from coming into the maturity you need to read and master the next chapter of your life. Own your stuff, say, "Yeah, I messed up—big time!" then get rid of stinkin' thinkin' and don't get stuck on stupid. Suck it up, strike a pose, and get on with it. Life is bigger than all the stuff you've been stressing over.

Then seize the day, girl! This is your moment to think outside the box and reinvent yourself, to do something you've never done before; it's the time to dig deep inside yourself and find the you that you've never met before—a resilient woman who has ideas she hasn't tried yet. Trust me, the possibilities are endless. So get out there and experiment; what have you got to lose? You've already lost it. Ha!

> *Decide to put away childish habits and mind-sets that keep you from coming into the maturity you need to read and master the next chapter of your life.*

Make friends with your creditors, and do the best you can. Don't give in to fear and intimidation. They can't squeeze blood from a turnip. They will take what you give them, believe me. So take it one day at a time. One dollar at a time, chip away at the old block until it's gone. Slow and steady wins the race.

In the meantime, stay beautiful. Stay positive. Stay prayerful and grateful. Put a smile on your face and a song in your heart. Nothing heals you like a good melody holding a promise of something good. Those are the only songs God writes. And you know a good song is worth its weight in gold.

Lastly, pursue a life well lived, and the wealth will come. See the big picture, and open yourself to receive it all. The Bible promises that the blessings of God will overtake you.[1] You just need to be in the right lane. So looking unto the Author and the Finisher of your faith, the One who holds all the things you need in His hands, run the race and know the rewards will meet you.[2]

It's the time to dig deep inside yourself and find the you that you've never met before—a resilient woman who has ideas she hasn't tried yet.

notes

Chapter 2: The Cold, Hard Facts
1. See Proverbs 29:18.
2. See Proverbs 27:23.

Chapter 3: Looking in the Rearview Mirror
1. See 1 John 2:16.
2. See Lamentations 1:9.

Chapter 4: Get Real, Girl!
1. See Habakkuk 2:2.
2. See Exodus 5.

Chapter 7: The Benefits of Plastic Surgery
1. See Proverbs 22:7.

Chapter 8: The Power of the Little Envelope and Loose Change
1. See Matthew 6:21.
2. See Hosea 4:6.

Chapter 9: How to Say No and Still Look Beautiful
1. See James 1:17.

Chapter 10: A Woman's Got to Have Priorities
1. 1 Timothy 6:10, KJV
2. See Matthew 6:24.
3. See Matthew 11:30.
4. See 3 John 1:2.

Chapter 11: The Fruit of Living Generously
1. See 2 Corinthians 9:7.
2. See Matthew 14:13-21.
3. See 2 Corinthians 9:10.

Chapter 13: The Secret of Community
1. See Acts 2:44-45.

Chapter 15: Ask and You Shall Receive, but Bartering Is Even Better
1. See Matthew 7:7-8.

Chapter 16: Puttin' On the Ritz and Other Creative Options
1. See Isaiah 52:1-3.

Chapter 21: The Secret to Self-Gratification
1. James 1:13, KJV

Chapter 23: There Is No Shame in Generics and Other Trade Secrets
1. See Exodus 4:1-5.

Chapter 29: Walmart, Tar-Jay, and Other Exotic Locales
1. See Proverbs 31:21, 25.

Chapter 30: Keep the Faith
1. See Romans 10:17.
2. See Philippians 4:19.
3. See Hosea 4:6.
4. James 1:2-4, *The Message*
5. See Romans 5:3-5.

Chapter 31: Ask Daddy
1. See Esther 4:16, KJV.
2. See Matthew 5:45.
3. See Psalm 37:25, KJV.
4. Psalm 91:14-16, *The Message*
5. See Job 1:21.

Chapter 32: Receive What You Believe
1. See Psalm 42:5.

Chapter 34: Final Diva Thoughts
1. See Deuteronomy 28:2, KJV.
2. See Hebrews 12:1-3.

additional resources

Budgeting Help
http://www.mvelopes.com/—Instead of spending money on a couple of lattes at the coffee shop, you can invest in this virtual envelope budgeting system. Mvelopes allows you to not only track your spending but track how much you have in savings.

Federal Reserve System
http://www.federalreserve.gov/consumerinfo/default.htm— This federal Web site has valuable consumer information, such as how to file a consumer complaint against a bank, what your credit report says about you, dealing with identity theft, looking for the best mortgage, and sixty-six ways to save money.

Affordable Housing Programs
http://www.makinghomeaffordable.gov/—Making Home Affordable is a plan to stabilize the housing market, part of the Obama administration's comprehensive Financial Stability Plan. This Web site provides homeowners with self-assessment tools and calculators to determine whether they might be eligible for a loan modification or a refinance under the administration's program, as well as other helpful resources and materials.

Learning about Money
http://www.mymoney.gov/—This is the federal government's Web site dedicated to helping Americans understand more about their money—how to save it, invest it, and manage it to meet their personal goals. You can use the resources on

this site to learn about budgeting, home ownership, paying for education, retirement planning, avoiding frauds and scams, starting a small business, and much more.

http://www.smartaboutmoney.org/—The National Endowment for Financial Education (NEFE) is an independent, nonprofit foundation committed to educating Americans on a broad range of financial topics and empowering them to make positive and sound decisions to reach their financial goals. The Web site offers tips on budgeting, reducing debt, setting financial goals, and other financial topics.

Veterans Affairs: U.S. Department of Veterans Affairs, Home Loan Guaranty Services

http://www.homeloans.va.gov/—This national Web site provides information on mortgage and loan options for veterans. The goal is to help veterans and active duty personnel purchase and retain homes in recognition of their service to the nation. The Web site is not just for veterans, however, as it has excellent information on buying, selling, or refinancing a home, as well as tips for first-time homebuyers.

Financial Planning for Generations X & Y

http://wiseupwomen.tamu.edu—This financial education Web site is a demonstration project targeted to women ages twenty-two to thirty-five, developed by the U.S. Department of Labor Women's Bureau. The online curriculum covers many topics, including financial planning, credit, insurance, and buying or leasing a car.

Biblically Based Financial Information

http://www.christianpf.com/the-best-christian-financial -websites—This collection offers you information on the top twenty Christian financial Web sites along with sources for all areas of financial concern.

http://crown.org—For a comprehensive course in budgeting, finance, investing, and saving, this is a great site to visit.

http://www.echristianfinance.com/—This Web site is a source for the fundamentals of budgeting and investing.

http://www.generousgiving.org—Do you need inspiration to give? Visit this Web site. It's a great way to learn about giving.

http://masteryourmoney.com/sample.asp—Financial advisor Ron Blue answers your questions on everything from dealing with debt to estate planning to retirement and taxes.

http://moralmoney.com/—This Web site offers tips for biblically responsible investing and stewardship.

about the author

AS A BEST-SELLING AUTHOR, speaker, singer, and inspiration to audiences all over the world, Michelle McKinney Hammond pinpoints the root causes of relational issues while sharing life-changing insights for "living, loving, and overcoming." It's Michelle's combination of grace, truth, transparency, and humor that has landed her in numerous media outlets, including *Essence* and *Ebony* magazines, the *Chicago Tribune*, and the *New York Times*, which called Michelle "the most visible face of the evangelical advice industry for single men and women."

Michelle has written thirty-four books and sold over two million copies worldwide. She also cohosted for ten years the Emmy Award–winning women's talk show *Aspiring Women*. Her numerous television appearances include *The Morning Show with Mike and Juliet* on Fox, *Politically Incorrect* with Bill Maher on ABC, *The Other Half* on NBC, *Baisden After Dark* on TV One, *Oh Drama!* on BET, *Soap Talk* on SOAPnet, *The 700 Club*, *The Morris Cerullo Show*, *Life Today with James Robison*, as well as appearances on Fox Chicago and *WGN Morning News* as the featured relationships expert.

additional books by michelle mckinney hammond

The Diva Principle
Get Over It and On With It
Release the Pain, Embrace the Joy
How to Be Blessed and Highly Favored
In Search of the Proverbs 31 Man
What Women Don't Know and Men Don't Tell You
What to Do Until Love Finds You
Secrets of an Irresistible Woman
How to Be Found by the Man You've Been Looking For
Sassy, Single, and Satisfied
How to Avoid the 10 Mistakes Single Women Make
The Power of Being a Woman
If Men Are Like Buses, Then How Do I Catch One?
Playing God
The Last Ten Percent
Why Do I Say "Yes" When I Need to Say "No"?
How to Make Love Work
How to Make Life Work
A Sassy Girl's Guide to Loving God

For more information or to contact Michelle McKinney Hammond, log on to **www.michellehammond.com**.